Dealing with Disappointment

Dealing *with*

Disappointment

Helping Kids Cope When Things Don't Go Their Way

by Elizabeth Crary

PARENTING PRESS, INC.

Seattle, Washington

Printed in the United States of America
Designed by Magrit Baurecht Design
Illustrations by Viki Woodworth

Library of Congress Cataloguing-in-Publication Data

Crary, Elizabeth, 1942-
    Dealing with disappointment / by Elizabeth Crary.
        p. cm.
    Includes bibliographical references.
    ISBN 1-884734-76-6 (library) – ISBN 1-884734-75-8 (paper)
    1. Child psychology. 2. Disappointment in children. 3. Emotions
in children. 4. Childrearing. I. Title.

    HQ772 .C73 2003
    649'.1–dc21

                                                    2002034586

Parenting Press, Inc.
P.O. Box 75267
Seattle, Washington 98125-0267

www.ParentingPress.com
Telephone 800-992-6657 • Fax 206-364-0702

Contents

1. Who's responsible for happiness? 7
2. What to do when your child is upset 14
3. What kids need to know about feelings 22
4. Self-calming tools 33
5. Problem-solving tools 43
6. Teaching both feelings and problem solving 56
7. Making changes 67
8. Staying calm when kids are upset 77
9. Questions and answers 94

Appendixes

A. The cost of emotional illiteracy 99
B. Activities for understanding feelings 101
C. Tools for coping with feelings 114
D. Songs and skits 125
E. Resources 129

Index 133

Teach about feelings
before tantrums begin.

Cultivate problem solving
before chaos sets in.

Chapter One

Who's responsible for happiness?

I can clearly remember the day I learned who was responsible for children's happiness. My husband and I got a babysitter for our six-month-old daughter and took our 6-year-old son Kevin to a special museum display he wanted very much to see.

The outing took six hours. And, except for one incident, we all had a grand time. As we drove up to our house, I asked him how he liked the trip. I fully expected him to say he was delighted since he had both parents' attention for more than six hours – doing something he wanted to do. However, he focused on the only five minutes in the trip that did not go exactly as he wished.

It was then I realized that my son was responsible for his happiness. Although I could provide wonderful experiences, ultimately I could not make him happy – only he could do that.

Who's responsible for children's happiness?

Matthew's having a fit because Mom won't give him a cookie now! Sara's whining because Dad won't let her watch more TV. And, Paul's upset because his homework is "too hard." What is a parent to do? Try to console your child, or shut yourself up in a soundproof room?

I don't know the answer for sure, but there is one thing that I am convinced of – you can't make another person happy. Ultimately that is his or her decision, as you see in the opening example above.

If you change activities to prevent or reduce your child's unhappiness, you encourage him to let another person (you) be responsible for his happiness. And if you rush to make life pleasant, you do not give your child the chance to develop the skills she needs to deal with her frustration and disappointment herself.

Parents' role. Although you cannot "make" your children happy, you do have an important role in making it possible for your children to choose happiness. You can help your children by modeling ways to deal with their feelings appropriately, by teaching your children the information and skills they need to choose happiness, and by backing out and letting children be responsible for their own feelings.

Children's role. The children's role is to notice their feelings, learn the skills they need to manage their feelings and the situations they face, to experiment to find what works for them, and to be active in choosing happiness.

Helping children learn to deal with disappointment not only makes it easier for them to choose happiness, but also helps protect them against some of the costs of emotional illiteracy.

Cost of emotional illiteracy. When children do not have the ability to soothe themselves, resolve their problems, and understand others' feelings, they are vulnerable to a host of problems – academic trouble, aggression, alcohol and drug addiction, depression, and eating disorders. These are briefly discussed in Appendix A.

The solution to emotional distress and illiteracy is not for the parent or teacher to make these children's lives emotionally smooth, but to give these children the skills they need to choose happiness and emotional competence.

ℐ〜 *What this book is about*

This book is about the tools and techniques that children need to cope with everyday issues. The focus is how you can teach your children to avoid, reduce, and eliminate the irritation from common childhood situations.

Dealing with Disappointment is a practical guide, not a research treatise or therapy. When your child acts angry, frustrated, and disappointed, you don't need to know exactly why he or she is upset to help, particularly since most of your child's learning occurs when your child is not upset.

We begin by looking at "what to do when your child is upset" because that is usually the first thing parents, teachers, and caregivers want to know. However, the bulk of the book is about what you do *between* upsets, because that is where change will happen – where you teach your child useful skills and strategies. *Dealing with Disappointment* offers you step-by-step directions for teaching skills and shows you how to change the way you interact with your child as he or she grows older. Finally, we look at how to cope with parental anger and conclude by answering a few common questions.

Each chapter offers you information, examples, and exercises. The information and examples help you understand what to do. The exercises let you practice using the ideas on your own before you try them with the kids.

Although the bulk of this book focuses on self-calming strategies and dealing with the situation, it is important to remember that anger and fear are sometimes warning signs that the person, child or adult, needs to leave the situation as fast as possible.

The more strategies you give your children today, the better prepared they will be for frustrations at home and in school, and for the more serious challenges they will confront later in life.

ᕳ What kids need to manage their feelings

Recently parents have begun to acknowledge their children's feelings and are surprised that their children sometimes remain upset. Acknowledging feelings is very helpful, and children need more than that. They need information about feelings, concrete tools and strategies to deal with their feelings and the situation they face, and support as they experiment and find what works for them.

Information about feelings. Kids need a feelings vocabulary, they need to know that feelings change, and that feelings are different from actions. This, and more, will be covered in Chapter 3.

Tool and strategies. Some children discover how to stay calm by themselves, and others grow into adulthood without the ability to truly calm themselves. These people can "put the lid on" their feelings. However, when things get stressful they often explode. In chapters 4 and 5 we will look at strategies or tools children can use to calm themselves and to deal with the situation, so they don't need to put the lid on their feelings.

Support. Children need different levels of parental support depending on their age and stage of learning. Sometimes support involves helping; other times support means giving the child time to use the tools and information he or she knows. We will address this in several chapters.

Support can also involve remaining calm when kids are upset and modeling appropriate ways to deal with your own feelings. We will look at things parents can do to keep calm in Chapter 8.

Some parents by their nature, experience, or temperament are more prepared to teach children about emotions. Other parents may handle their feelings well, but do it inside themselves so their children do not know how their parents deal with their feelings. Once these parents learn what children need, they can easily adapt. Still other parents may need information or support themselves before they can address their children's needs. In the next section you can look at how parents typically respond to children's feelings.

How do you handle kids' feelings?

One way you can help your children choose happiness is to provide the information and support they need. To do that, it is helpful to understand how you commonly respond to kids' feelings.

Some parents grew up in caring households; others in critical households. Some people hope to emulate their parents; others vow never to repeat their parents' mistakes. Exercise 1-1: "What is your parenting EQ (emotional quotient) style?" is intended to help you identify how you handle children's feelings. Exercise 1-2 explains how to interpret your responses. That exercise also suggests what your child may need.

As you read this book, you may find ways you could do things differently. It is my intention to increase your options rather than to burden you. I hope that you think about the material you find relevant. You can take one or two ideas and try them. If they work, or even if they don't work, you can come back and try something else.

In this chapter we have looked at who is responsible for happiness, some things children need, and how you handle kids' feelings. The key to helping your child deal with disappointment is to provide information, skills, and support. However, one of the first questions many parents ask is, "What do I do when my child is upset?" In the next chapter we will look at what you can do when your child has a meltdown.

Exercise 1-1:
What is your parenting EQ style?

Instructions: Read the situation and circle the letter of the answer that most closely resembles how you would respond. (Explanation in Exercise 1-2)

1. **You are walking down the street with 2-year-old Allie. As you approach a fenced yard, the dog starts to bark loudly. Allie begins to cry and you –**
   a. Immediately pick her up and comfort her, saying, "Mommy won't let that mean dog get you."
   b. Speak firmly, "Stop crying! The dog can't hurt you. He's behind the fence."
   c. Say, "Come, let's walk on the other side of the street."
   d. Say, "Wow, that dog sounds scary. Would you feel safer if I hold your hand or carry you?"

2. **Blake (age 4) was building a block tower. Charlie (age 2) tried to put a block on top and accidently knocked the tower over. Blake was furious. He yelled at Charlie. Before Blake does anything more, you –**
   a. Say, "I'm so sorry Charlie knocked over your tower. You must be really disappointed. You worked so hard. Come, I'll read you a story."
   b. Tell him to be quiet, "Blake, silence! You're making a mountain out of a mole hill. There is no need to get upset about every little thing that happens."
   c. Say quietly, "Charlie didn't mean to knock the tower down. Come, I'll help you rebuild it."
   d. Say, "It looks like you're angry Charlie knocked your tower down. Would you like to tell me about it or run around the yard to calm yourself?"

3. **Dawn (age 5) was absently licking an ice cream cone as she watched the monkeys at the zoo. When the scoop of ice cream fell on the ground, Dawn began to cry. You say –**
   a. "Oh, dear. You're upset your ice cream fell on the ground. Strawberry is your favorite flavor. (You look around.) Oh, look, Dawn, that monkey is swinging by his tail. Isn't he silly?"
   b. "Dawn, be quiet! How many times have I told you to watch what you're doing? If you had watched what you were doing, this would not have happened."
   c. "Hush, Dawn. We can go get another ice cream cone. This time you can have two scoops."
   d. "Oh, dear. You're upset that your ice cream fell on the ground. Would you like to take a deep breath to calm yourself or would a hug help?"

continued on page 12

4. Ellen came home from school crying, "Francie didn't invite me to her birthday party Saturday." You –

a. Sit beside her and say, "You feel hurt Francie didn't invite you to her party. It's okay, Sweetie, you have other friends. Let's think about something else. Shall we bake some cookies?"

b. Say, "Calm down, Ellen – it's only a party. Tell me, what did you do to make her mad at you?"

c. Say enthusiastically, "Let's call Sierra right now and see if she can play Saturday. You two can do something really fun."

d. Comment, "It really hurts when a friend doesn't invite you to a party. It often helps to remember that you are a good person, even when a friend is mean. What do you think will help the pain pass? Drawing a picture of your feelings? Reading a book? Or, making a silly dance?"

5. George wanted to be the pirate in the class play. He has been practicing the lines. You asked him if he got the part when he came home today. He said, "No," and then started to tease his sister. You –

a. Say, "You must be disappointed. You practiced and practiced and you didn't get the part. I'll tell you what, let's go order pizza for supper tonight. What kind would you like?"

b. Say emphatically, "Leave Hanna alone! Just because you didn't get a part in the play doesn't give you a right to hurt her. You know better than that."

c. Say, "Forget about the class play, George. Acting classes start Saturday. Then you can be in a real play."

d. Gently say, "It's okay to be upset that you didn't get the part, and you may not tease your sister. You need to find another way to feel better. Do you want help thinking of ideas?"

6. Isabel is a bright, articulate girl. To qualify for the school math team, she had to get a 95% on the math test today. The minute she walks in after school you know she didn't make it. You –

a. Open your arms to give her a hug. Say, "Isabel, I'm so-o-o sad. You wanted to be on the math team with Jenny. I have an idea, you can take gymnastics with her. Let's call her now."

b. Say, "Isabel, don't sulk! There is no point letting the world know your feelings. Beside, you should be happy you didn't make the team. Now you don't have all those practices."

c. Say, "Isabel, I read this interesting article on the debate team. I think you should join the debate team. You're a natural for debate."

d. Say, "You look disappointed. Let me guess, you didn't make 95% on the math test, right? I know how much it meant to you. Is there anything I can do to help?"

Exercise 1-2:
Identifying your parenting EQ style

....

Instructions: Count the number of responses for each letter and put them in the appropriate boxes below. Then read the description of the response.

....

A's demonstrate a *Sensitive response.* Parent notices the child's distress, acknowledges his or her feelings and often tries to distract the child. However, the parent does not offer tools (or strategies) for dealing with the feelings and rarely sets limits on the child's behavior because the child will be more unhappy.

B's illustrate a *Critical response.* Parent dismisses or discounts the child's feelings and may criticize the child for exhibiting feelings. These parents may also blame the child for the situation. They do not offer skills to handle the feelings. These parents often dislike any display of feeling. They may need to become more comfortable with overt feelings to help their children.

C's show a *Fixing response.* Parents solve the child's problem or avoid the situation so the child won't be upset. They rarely acknowledge feelings, or offer tools to deal with the feeling itself, or encourage the child to solve the problem by himself or herself.

D's demonstrate a *Coaching response.* Parents acknowledge the child's feelings and offer strategies the child can use to deal with the feelings. As children learn the strategies, these parents remind them that they have choices and that they (the parents) are available as a resource.

Chapter Two

What to do when your child is upset

When children have tantrums or meltdowns parents want to know what to do "now." The good news is there are things you can do to help your child to deal with his feelings over time. The bad news is that nothing "works" in the moment of "crisis." Once your child has "lost it," he can rarely learn anything until he is calm again.

At the moment of crisis, the most effective approach is to give the child the support he needs, and then plan what you will teach him when he is calm.

In this chapter we will look at four levels of support and how to respond to children both when they are upset and before their next disappointment.

Levels of support

Children need different support at different ages or at least different stages of emotional development. The following is an example of a young child who has already been taught to deal with his feelings.

Andy (2¾) had trouble going to sleep. The wind pounded the house and the electricity had gone out, so he didn't have his usual night light. During the night, power was restored and Andy awakened to see a bear shadow on his ceiling. His mom heard his frightened cries and comforted him. "You saw shadows on the walls and were scared." When he was calm, she offered him several things he might do to feel safer. He chose to keep his light on the rest of the night.

For the next several days, he would review the night experience. "The trees banged the house. It was dark. I woke up and a bear was in my room." Each time he repeated the story, Mom would say, "You were scared by the bear shadows. What did you do to feel safe?"

When Andy's grandad heard the story, he said, "I'll take care of that for you." He charged into the bedroom, picked up a teddy bear and tossed it on Andy's bed. "That's the problem," he said (pointing to the bear). "The bear's gone now. You don't need to be scared." For the rest of Grandad's visit, Andy stayed near one of his parents.

When Grandad left, Mom asked Andy what was the matter. He replied sadly, "He didn't understand." Then he brightened slightly and added, "You understand. Daddy understands."

When children are young, they need to have their feelings labeled – just the way we label colors, trees, and animals. When you reflect the feeling and the situation to young children, you help children in two ways. First, you give children language to use about their feelings. Second, you help children separate the feelings from actions or the situation.

While children are learning about feelings, it is appropriate for parents (and caregivers) to offer a child ways to deal with his or her feelings. For example, when Sarah is upset because Dad is leaving, you might offer, "Would you like me to read you a story or give you a hug?" Or, when Tyrone is angry because he can't have a cookie, you can offer, "Would you like a cracker now or a cookie for dessert?"

Transition. When children are young, it is appropriate to comfort them, to give them a hug or to kiss away an "owie." However, as children grow, they need to become responsible for their feelings – to find ways to express them appropriately. When a parent or caregiver always "makes it better," the child does not learn the skills to make himself or herself happy.

Parents' role changes as children grow

Parent role:	Comforter	Teacher	Coach	Supporter
Message for child:	I will take care of you.	You have choices.	You can think of choices.	You are in charge. I'll support you.
Example: Child is scared of a dog.	Parent picks up the scared child and calms her.	Parent asks, "Would you like to hold my hand or be carried?"	Parent asks, "What can you do to feel safe?"	Parent says, "Let me know if I can help you."

There is no magic age when you suddenly stop comforting a child and expect her to take charge. Instead, gradually turn responsibility for dealing with feelings over to the child. You begin by comforting the child, then offering choices, then reminding the child she has options, then backing off and offering support. You can see how support works with older children and teens in the following story.

Toni came home from school, slammed the front door, yelled at the dog, and stomped into the kitchen to get a snack. Mom looked up from her work at the table and observed blandly, "I heard you slam the door and stomp to the kitchen. I'm wondering if you're upset about something that happened at school today." Toni made no rely. "Well," Mom continued, "I'll be here most of this afternoon if you want me for anything" and returned to her work.

After rattling and banging things in the kitchen for a bit longer, Toni plopped down near Mom and launched into a litany of how stupid Mr. Smyth was. "He couldn't even recognize a correct answer if it bit him." Mom acknowledged her comments with "Um," "Oh," or "Really?" After a while Toni calmed down and said, "I guess I should go talk to Mr. Smyth after class tomorrow."

Older children. When children have the skills to identify and deal with their feelings, parents and caregivers need to move to the role of observer and supporter. It would be foolish to say to an older child, "You're angry about something that happened at school." Teens' feelings are so complex it is difficult to know if the problem is with the grade, the teacher, the students in the class, or something else entirely. Further, you offer unsolicited advice or choices at your peril. If you said, "You can write Mr. Smyth a letter or ask to see the principal," you would probably elicit a "Boy, are you stupid!"

Teens need acceptance of their feelings and support while they think things through *themselves*. When parents or caregivers label feelings or offer choices for the situation, teens often feel put down. The very responses that are helpful with younger children are insulting to teens.

Acknowledging feelings involves accepting people's feelings and supporting them while they deal with the feelings and situation. The form that the support takes depends on the skills of the child. Parents and caregivers need to tune into the child's ability rather than his or her age. For example, when teens have not learned appropriate skills, they need information before they can make wise choices. And young children who understand feelings (like Andy in the opening example) need to have their ability respected.

ℐ Younger and unskilled children

We are going to look at handling kids' feelings in two parts: first during the moment of crisis, and, second, before the next crisis.

During the crisis. When kids are upset it is rarely a crisis, although it often feels that way. The first thing to do is ensure the safety of people and things. When everything is safe, acknowledge the child's feelings; set the limits, if needed; and offer the child choices and support.

Offering support may be tricky. Some children want to be left alone, others feel abandoned if you leave. You can ask what the child wants, but remember that she may not really know. You may need to experiment to see what works best.

Learning rarely takes place when a person is upset, because it is hard to think logically. However, how you handle the situation tells your child what behavior is appropriate when he is upset. You can see these steps in the charts below.

Situation: Brianna and her dad went to the park where she loved to swing. She waited for a turn but did not get one before she had to leave. When she got home, she started tearing the pages from a book.

Step	Starter ideas	Example
Check for safety	Move anyone or anything being hurt.	Put the book up.
Acknowledge feelings	"It's okay to feel _____."	"Brianna, it is okay to be upset, . . ."
Set limits	"And I will not let you _____."	"And I will not let you damage the book."
Offer choices	"You may ____ or _____ instead."	"You may draw a picture or shake out your anger."
Offer support*	"Would you like me to _____?"	"Would you like me to sit near you?"

*Note: If Brianna says, "No. I don't want you," Dad could say, "Okay," then sit in the same room but not nearby.

When you acknowledge a child's feeling, the child may or may not begin to calm down. However, the approach is helpful even if the child remains upset. It tells the child that feelings are acceptable and helps her distinguish between feelings and actions. It also says you care about her and trust her to deal with her feelings.

Children are sensitive to the feelings of their caregiver. It is helpful when you can maintain a patient attitude in spite of their histrionics. Your calmness can help them calm down eventually, but not necessarily quickly. You can practice dealing with a crisis in Exercise 2-1.

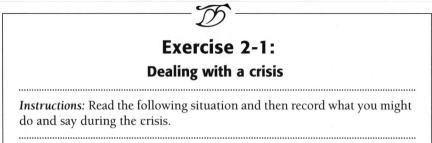

Exercise 2-1:
Dealing with a crisis

Instructions: Read the following situation and then record what you might do and say during the crisis.

Situation: Joel, 7 years old, storms into the living room hunting for his younger brother. Joel has just discovered that Jerry has dripped chocolate ice cream on his baseball card. "I'm going to drip chocolate syrup all over your new book," he yells at his brother.

Step	Starter ideas	Example
Check for safety	Move anyone or anything being hurt.	
Acknowledge feelings	"It's okay to feel _____."	
Set limits	"And I will not let you _____."	
Offer choices	"You may _____ or _____ instead."	
Offer support	"Would you like me to _____?"	

Possible answer: Check for safety: Nothing and no one is being hurt yet. Say to Joel, "It's okay to be mad at Jerry, and it is not okay to damage his book. You may tell him how you feel or ask him how he will fix the situation. If you want, I can help him think of ways to resolve the situation."

Between crises. If you only deal with feelings at crisis time, your child will probably continue to have emotional meltdowns. That is because although acknowledging feelings is helpful, it does not teach the child *how* to manage his or her feelings or the situation. Begin with these three actions.

Teach new strategies. Decide what skills or information your child needs to handle his feelings more appropriately. The "Skills inventory" on page 28 may give you ideas. You can introduce concepts by modeling them, reading stories, or making up games. Appendix B provides activities to understand feelings, and Appendix C demonstrates how to teach calming techniques to children.

Acknowledge children's effort. When children learn a new skill, it is a gradual process. Learning to cope with feelings may take weeks or months, rather than hours or days. When you look for and comment on your child's effort, it helps both you and your child when you notice that change is happening.

Reduce stress. Children are under a lot of stress. The stress could be from the child's experiences, like a move, a new sibling, trouble at school, worrying about the health of a relative, or parents' quarreling. Or the stress could be secondhand stress – picked up from other people in the child's life.

When the child's "stress bucket" overflows, the child has few reserves to deal with the inevitable daily disappointments. If your child's life is stressful, it helps to reduce what stress you can so he can concentrate on learning about feelings. This might mean reducing the number of activities a child is involved in, spending more one-on-one time with your child, or dealing with your own stress.

You will see how Brianna's dad planned to help her deal with feelings in general as we continue with the steps for handling feelings below.

Goal	Plan	Example
Teach needed skills	I will teach her to calm herself by modeling taking deep breaths.	"I'm so angry. I'm going to take three deep breaths." Breathe, breathe, breathe. "Oh, I'm still upset. I'll take two more breaths." Breathe. Breathe. "Ahh. I feel better now."
Acknowledge feelings	I will watch and praise her when she tries to take deep breaths.	"Wow, you remembered to take a deep breath."
Reduce stress	She has a lot of activities. I think I will reduce them.	When this gymnastics session is over, I won't renew the class. We can stay home and play games together.

Often parents acknowledge the child's tantrums and help the child calm down, then wonder why the child is still having tantrums months or years later. One reason is that although the child has a good feelings vocabulary, he or she has no skills for self-soothing and no skills to deal with the specific situation. In Exercise 2-2 you can continue to make a

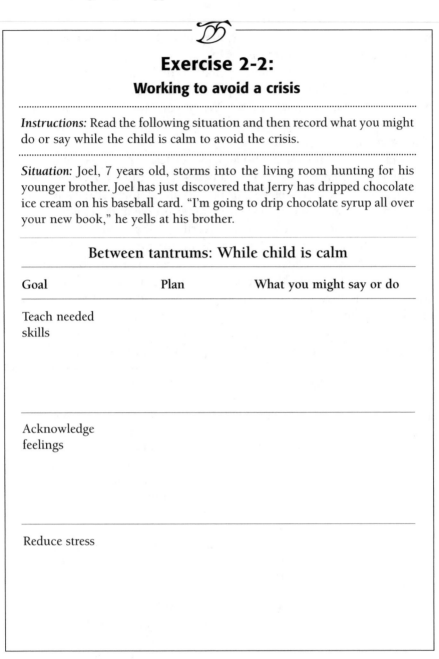

Exercise 2-2:
Working to avoid a crisis

Instructions: Read the following situation and then record what you might do or say while the child is calm to avoid the crisis.

Situation: Joel, 7 years old, storms into the living room hunting for his younger brother. Joel has just discovered that Jerry has dripped chocolate ice cream on his baseball card. "I'm going to drip chocolate syrup all over your new book," he yells at his brother.

Between tantrums: While child is calm

Goal	Plan	What you might say or do
Teach needed skills		
Acknowledge feelings		
Reduce stress		

plan to help Joel (see Exercise 2-1). And in Exercise 2-3 you can take a situation you face with a child and use the steps to develop a plan.

If you want your children to be emotionally competent, you must teach them about the nature of feelings, self-calming techniques, and how to resolve problems. We will look at each of these in the next three chapters.

Exercise 2-3:
Dealing with a tantrum

Instructions: Think about a time when your child was upset and describe the situation briefly. Then record what you might say during the crisis and later while the child is calm.

Your situation:

_____

During the crisis

Step	Starter ideas	What you might say
Check for safety	Move anyone or anything being hurt.	
Acknowledge feelings	"It's okay to feel _____."	
Set limits	"And I will not let you _____."	
Offer choices	"You may ____ or _____ instead."	
Offer support	"Would you like me to _____?"	

Between tantrums: While child is calm

Goal	Plan	What you might say or do
Teach needed skills		
Acknowledge feelings		
Reduce stress		

Chapter Three

What kids need to know about feelings

Everyone has feelings whether they express them or suppress them. Before people can cope effectively with their feelings, it is helpful to understand the nature of feelings.

What kids need to know can be divided into three parts: how to identify feelings, the nature of feelings, and, how to cope with feelings.

How to identify feelings

Children need a feelings vocabulary to communicate their emotions. They also need to know what those feelings feel like physically. And, they need to know how to identify feelings in others.

Vocabulary. People need a variety of words to describe how they feel. Most people use only a few words. For fun, take a minute (yes, 60 seconds) and write down all the feelings words you can think of in Exercise 3-1.

You can introduce vocabulary in many ways. You can label your feelings, "I'm frustrated that I can't get the drawer to open. Something must be stuck." You can observe feelings of others. For example, in the mall you can comment, "Look how tired that woman is. Her shoulders are drooping and she is trudging along." And you can label children's feelings, "You're sad that you can't go shopping with your sister." Or, "You're excited that we are going to the zoo today."

You can also use books to introduce feelings. *The Way I Feel* by Janan Cain is a wonderful book with strong pictures that kids can identify with even if they don't know the names of the feelings. You can ask children to name the feeling, tell them a time you felt that way, or ask them when they felt that way.

You can also watch a video with your child and stop the tape to ask the child how the character feels. When you comment on feelings, use a wide variety of feelings words.

Exercise 3-1:
Feelings vocabulary

Instructions: Set a timer for 60 seconds and list all the feelings words you can think of below. When you are done, follow the bulleted directions.

_____	_____
_____	_____
_____	_____
_____	_____
_____	_____
_____	_____
_____	_____
_____	_____

- Put a check mark in front of all the comfortable words.
- Count the comfortable words and record the number: ____ .
- Record the total number of words: ____ .

Comment: Generally the first time people do this exercise only about one quarter of the words they list are "comfortable" emotions. Repeat the exercise and aim for about half comfortable feelings words.

Variety. When you label feelings for your children, label both comfortable and uncomfortable feelings. Many parents notice and comment on feelings only when they themselves are concerned or irritated. "You're scared of the dog." "You're mad at your sister." Rarely do parents say, "You look contented sitting there with your book." Reflecting only on uncomfortable feelings can encourage children to notice and feel more uncomfortable feelings, at the expense of comfortable ones. So, include a variety of feelings – mad, happy, scared, content, irritated, elated, frustrated, proud. For more words to use check the list on page 24.

101 Feelings words

These words reflect both comfortable and uncomfortable feelings. Add your own feelings words and introduce some of them into your conversation.

Comfortable	Dreamy	Happy	Resilient
Accepted	Eager	Inspired	Resistant
Accomplished	Ecstatic	Interested	Ridiculous
Affectionate	Elated	Joyous	Romantic
Ambivalent	Excited	Loved	Satisfied
Calm	Exuberant	Loving	Secure
Cared for	Fanciful	Mellow	Self-confident
Comfortable	Fantastic	Mild	Silly
Compassionate	Friendly	Mystified	Surprised
Confident	Generous	Okay	Thoughtful
Content	Giggly	Pleased	Thrilled
Curious	Glad	Proud	Wondering
Delighted	Good	Relaxed	

Uncomfortable	Disappointed	Indignant	Sad
Afraid	Embarrassed	Irate	Sheepish
Angry	Enraged	Irritated/Irked	Shy
Annoyed	Exasperated	Jealous	Terrified
Anxious	Forlorn	Left out	Thwarted
Apathetic	Frustrated	Lonely	Uncomfortable
Bored	Furious	Nervous	Unsatisfied
Chagrined	Flabbergasted	Overwhelmed	Unsure
Cheated	Greedy	Peeved	Upset
Confused	Grumpy	Put upon	Worried
Defiant	Guilty	Reckless	
Dejected	Horrified	Regretful	
Depressed	Hostile	Rejected	
Disagreeable	Hurt	Scared	

Gradations. Children need to recognize mild, moderate, and intense feelings. When you use a wide spectrum of feelings words, you teach your child to notice the gentle feelings as well as the dramatic ones. If you notice when your child is mildly upset, you can offer coping strategies that the child would reject when she is very upset. Also, when you acknowledge mild feelings, the child may be able to try coping strategies herself because she is not so upset. In Exercise 3-2 on page 25 you can practice thinking of gradations of feelings.

Exercise 3-2:
Identify graded feelings

Instructions: Fill in the mild and intense feeling words that correspond to the moderate word given. There are several possible answers for each word.

Feeling

Mild	Moderate	Intense
_____	Happy	_____
_____	Angry	_____
_____	Scared	_____

Possible answers: content – happy – exited; annoyed – angry – furious; worried/anxious – scared – terrified.

Internal signs of feelings. The human body reacts to what a person is feeling. Children need to learn to notice these physical signs of feelings in their bodies. Take a moment and think of how your body feels when you experience certain feelings – hot, cold, tense, relaxed, explosive, etc. You can record your thoughts for some emotions in Exercise 3-3.

When you are happy, your body probably feels warm and relaxed. When you are angry, you may feel hot, muscles may tense, and you probably feel an explosive energy. When people are sad, they describe their bodies as feeling cool and having low energy. People who are depressed feel a relentless, overwhelming tiredness.

It is helpful for children to learn to notice the feelings in their bodies because these sensations can help them figure out what is happening. If someone asks, "Are you mad?" they can look inside. If they find their muscles tense and red hot, they can reflect on when they started to feel that way. This may give them insight into what they are angry about.

Some people have slipped into the habit of ignoring or suppressing their feelings. Over time, they may forget how to notice what is happening inside. When that happens, people (children or adults) lose a valuable source of information.

Exercise 3-3:
Notice how emotions feel

Instructions: Read each word. Think about how that emotion feels in your body – hot, cold, heavy, light, tight, loose, tense, relaxed, etc. Then record your body's feelings in the space provided.

Happy

_____

Sad

_____

Angry

_____

Proud

_____

Scared

ᥱ *The nature of feelings*

Children who understand the nature of feelings are better able to handle both their feelings and those of other people.

Feelings are okay. For some children emotions are confusing. They have emotional energy swirling around in their bodies and they don't understand what it is or what to do with it. They may think that the feelings are bad. We need to help children know that all feelings are acceptable, and that the feelings can be expressed in helpful or hurtful ways.

Feelings change. Most children live in the present. They believe that the way they feel now is the way they will always feel. It is helpful for them to understand that they can be sad now and happy later. Just because a friend was mad this morning does not mean she will be mad this afternoon. In the example below, Erik was able to calm himself because he knew that feelings change.

Erik asked his brother Kevin to play ball. Kevin said no, he had to read his history assignment. Erik started to cry, but remembered that Kevin might change his mind later and play.

Ten minutes later he returned and asked, "Would you like to play now?"
"Sure," Kevin replied, "I finished the chapter."

Feelings are different from actions. Children need to know that "It is okay to be angry, and it's not okay to hurt someone or something."

The simplest way to teach the difference is repetition. "I know you love the cat, and you may not squeeze her so hard. It hurts her." Or, "You're curious about the glass bird, and you may not touch it." Or, "It looks like you're frustrated that your block tower keeps falling down, and you may not kick the blocks around. Something could get damaged."

When you reflect the feeling and the situation, you help children distinguish between them. In the following example, three-and-a-half-year-old Megan told her mother about an incident at preschool.

"Brian was mean at school today. He knocked down my tower. I was mad. I wanted to push him so hard he fell off the world."

Mom responded, "Wow, sounds like you were really mad. What did you do?"

Megan answered, "Oh, I built it up again."

Feelings can be expressed in many ways. Young children often express their feelings by crying, screaming, pushing, biting, or hitting. Over time they can learn that there are other ways to demonstrate their feelings. One way you can teach alternatives is to model constructive behavior and verbalize what you are doing. This is illustrated below.

Mom is looking at the mess on the floor. "I'm really upset that I dropped the carton of eggs. I'm going to take three deep breaths and see if I feel calmer." She takes the breaths and then checks to see if she is still mad. "I'm still mad. I'm going to take three more breaths." Again she breathes and checks in with herself. This time she might say, "Yes, I feel calmer now."

Children need to learn a variety of ways to respond and then to decide which will work best in each situation. When you model various ways of calming yourself, you are helping them to learn ways to calm themselves. We will focus on self-calming techniques and strategies in Chapter 4.

Feelings vary from person to person. People feel differently about the same things. Even though research shows that children as young as 18 months can realize that feelings vary, they generally assume that other people feel exactly as they do. Because of their egocentrism, it surprises them that another child likes chocolate ice cream while they hate it. This surprise carries over into the social realm as well, as you can see in the example below.

Nora, age 6, was an intense child. Her parents had been working with her to help her moderate her response and to problem solve differences. Nora wanted to play with her older brother, Matt.

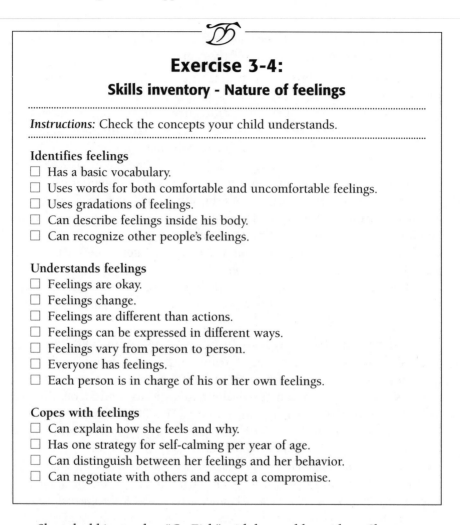

Exercise 3-4:
Skills inventory - Nature of feelings

Instructions: Check the concepts your child understands.

Identifies feelings
- ☐ Has a basic vocabulary.
- ☐ Uses words for both comfortable and uncomfortable feelings.
- ☐ Uses gradations of feelings.
- ☐ Can describe feelings inside his body.
- ☐ Can recognize other people's feelings.

Understands feelings
- ☐ Feelings are okay.
- ☐ Feelings change.
- ☐ Feelings are different than actions.
- ☐ Feelings can be expressed in different ways.
- ☐ Feelings vary from person to person.
- ☐ Everyone has feelings.
- ☐ Each person is in charge of his or her own feelings.

Copes with feelings
- ☐ Can explain how she feels and why.
- ☐ Has one strategy for self-calming per year of age.
- ☐ Can distinguish between her feelings and her behavior.
- ☐ Can negotiate with others and accept a compromise.

She asked him to play "Go Fish" with her and he said no. She got upset and demanded, "You have to!"

Matt asked, "Why do I have to?" "Because I want to," she answered. "Well, I don't want to," he responded.

Nora was about to lose what little control she had when she remembered that people feel differently about things. She asked, "What would you rather play?" "I'd rather play 'Checkers,'" he replied. "Okay," Nora beamed as she ran to get the game.

Everyone has feelings. Since children cannot see or feel people's feelings in the way they see and feel objects, children often conclude that other people do not have feelings.

You can help by labeling other people's feelings and then asking children to guess how others feel. For example, "Sue is happy because she can go with us." "Matt is frustrated because he has to wait until tomorrow for

Paul to come over." "Maria is jumping up and down. How do you think she is feeling?" "Dad's shoulders are drooping. How do you think he feels?"

You can help children understand that all people have feelings by talking about your own feelings, both comfortable and uncomfortable, and commenting on your observations of other people's feelings.

∾ *How to cope with feelings*

When children are upset there are two aspects – the feeling itself and the situation or event that preceded the feeling. Children need tools or strategies to deal with both these aspects. You can see these aspects in the following example.

Annika came home from school sobbing. She hadn't won a blue ribbon in the track meet. She threw her books aside, knocking over the lamp, and pushed her sister off the sofa so she could lie there and cry.

Annika's feeling was intense disappointment and the situation was not winning a blue ribbon. She needs to be able to release her feelings in an appropriate manner – not hurt her sister or the lamp. And she needs to consider her options for the next meet. We will be looking at ways to cope with the feelings in Chapter 4 and ways to handle the situation in Chapter 5.

∾ *How can you teach these concepts?*

In an ideal world children would be born with a feelings vocabulary, an understanding of feelings, and knowledge of how to cope with them. However, this is not the case. We must teach these concepts. Four ways to teach are modeling, observations, stories, and activities.

Modeling. You can share your feelings. "This is the third red light in a row. I'm frustrated." Or, "I asked my boss for someone to help on this new project. He said he didn't have anyone free. I'm really disappointed."

Observations. You can comment on how your feelings change. For example, when you complain that the checkbook doesn't balance, and then finally balance it, you can remark, "Feelings change. Remember a bit ago I was really upset when I couldn't make the checkbook balance? Now I feel better."

When a child's balloon floats away, it does not do any good to tell him, "Relax, soon you'll forget about it." However, later when he is calm, you can remark, "You feel calm now. Earlier you were upset that your balloon blew away. Isn't it interesting the way feelings change so often."

You can also comment on change you see while you are out. For example, in the park you could say, "Look, the little girl feels better now. Remember how she was crying when her sand castle fell down? I guess her feelings changed."

You can also comment on how people your child knows feel differently about the same thing. For example, "Isn't it funny that we are all afraid of some things and not afraid of other things? I'm afraid of high places. You're scared of dogs. And, Daddy's afraid of snakes. But, I'm not scared of snakes and you're not scared of heights and Daddy's not afraid of dogs."

Stories. When you read stories or watch videos with your child, you can comment on how the character's feelings change. For example, in the book *All My Feelings at Home: Ellie's Day* by Susan Levine Friedman and Susan Conlin, Ellie goes through many feelings. You can also use regular story books and comment on what is happening. There is more about using stories to teach about feelings in Appendix B.

Activities. You can make up games to help children understand emotional concepts. For example, you could make a "feelings dial" by drawing lines on a paper plate, dividing it into six sections (see page 105). In each section, draw a face with a different emotion. Then ask your child to point to how he or she feels. Later you can ask again. This helps children identify their feelings and also to notice that feelings change. Again, there are more ideas in Appendix B.

We have looked at four ways to teach children about feelings: modeling, commenting, using stories, and doing activities. You also teach by how you respond to your child's distress. Sometimes grown-ups unconsciously dismiss children's feelings.

ℰ *Blocking children's emotional development*

Some parents want their children to know that feelings are okay; at the same time, they do not want to deal with their children's feelings. These parents give the message that "Feelings are okay, but not really." There are four ways parents unknowingly discount children's feelings: denying, reducing, dismissing, and solving them. These discounts are described and illustrated briefly in the following chart.

Situations:	Kathy came home from school crying because Molly said her dress was ugly.	Brian's sister tore his favorite book. He ran to Mom saying, "I hate Lizzie. She tore my book."
Denying	"You're not upset. You don't care what Molly thinks of your dress."	"You don't hate your sister. You love her."
Reducing	"She's not mean. I'm sure you misunderstood her."	"You don't hate her. You are just a little annoyed."

continued on page 31

| Dismissing | "Well, what do you expect when you wear your old clothes." | "Well, she wouldn't have torn it if you had put it away properly." |
| Solving | "Let's go out and buy you some new dresses." | "Get me the tape and I'll fix it for you." |

Each of these examples negates the child's feeling. Denying says you are wrong, you do not feel that way. Reducing says you are overreacting, you shouldn't feel that strongly. Dismissing says it is not reasonable for you to feel that way. And, solving discounts the feeling by fixing it rather than accepting it.

Instead of blocking or dismissing the feelings, you can acknowledge the feeling without judging or agreeing, as seen in the chart below.

Simple listening	Simply listen to Kathy. Say, "Oh," "Really," "Umm" where appropriate.	Listen to Brian's distress. Comment, "Umm." "Really?" "I see" where appropriate.
Acknowledge the feeling	"You're sad that Molly didn't like your dress."	"You're really upset Lizzie tore your favorite book."
Offer help	"You're angry that Molly didn't like your outfit. Is there any way I can help?"	"You're angry that Lizzie tore your favorite book. Would you like me to do something?"

Each of the comments above tells the child that his or her feelings are okay and also leaves the responsibility for dealing with the feeling to the child.

ℐ Questions & answers

I ignore feelings like boredom and jealousy because I don't want to encourage those feelings. Is that okay?

That depends. If you want your child to be ignorant of the *words* to describe her feelings, it will work. However, if you do not want the child to experience the feelings of boredom or jealousy, ignoring the feelings will not work. The child will still have the same feelings, but will learn to label them as anger, frustration, or something else. Many people believe it is helpful to use the most accurate word because it is easier to figure out how to handle the situation if they know what they are really feeling.

Doesn't labeling their feelings tell children what they are feeling? What if you're wrong?

Labeling feelings is important because it helps children understand that the feeling is a natural part of living. If you mislabel fear as anger, the feeling will not change, any more than calling a rose a daisy will make it a daisy.

Unless you and other people all mislabel the same feelings, the errors won't make any difference. If the child is unfamiliar with the word, he doesn't usually learn the meaning until he has heard it several times. If the child knows the name of his feeling and you mislabel the feeling, he will tell you, "No! I'm not sad Allen isn't coming – I'm mad. He promised to bring his new transformer and now I have to wait."

In this chapter we have looked at what information and skills children need to deal with their disappointment. In the next chapter we will look at six groups of self-calming tools and how to teach those techniques to children.

Chapter Four

Self-calming tools

Everyone needs self-calming tools, children and parents alike. The good news is that skills are teachable. The bad news is that teaching takes time.

Children begin to learn to soothe themselves as babies. With luck and help, they will continue to learn more ways to calm themselves as they grow. It is my belief that if a child cannot calm herself down in most situations by age four, you need to deliberately teach her calming skills.

Often, when a child is upset, the parent will rush in and fix the situation – distract the child, buy her a new balloon, or mend the toy. This may make your child happy now, but your lose the opportunity to teach the child how to make herself happy in the future. If this continues, your child will become dependent on others for happiness, rather than learn to deal with her situations herself.

In this chapter we will look at six groups of self-calming tools, a process to teach those tools, and four levels of support for children's feelings.

Six groups of self-calming tools

Most children have a natural or preferred mode of expressing feelings often related to their temperament. It may be verbal (crying), physical (hitting), visual (watching trees sway), or something else. Sometimes your child's natural mode is enough to calm him down; other times it may not be suitable to the situation.

As you consider what tools to teach your child to calm himself, think both present and future. When children are young physical activities, like running or stomping, often work best. However, these strategies will be less helpful in the boardroom as an adult. Take a moment to list the ways you or other family members calm down in Exercise 4-1.

Children need a variety of tools to calm themselves. I suggest that children have at least one tool per year of age. That means a two-year-old needs two tools. A five-year-old needs five tools. There are six groups of tools that you can teach your child: physical, auditory/verbal, visual, creative, self-comforting, and humor.

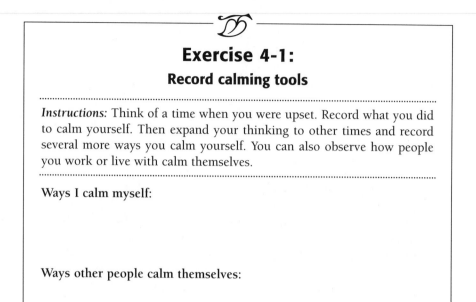

Exercise 4-1:
Record calming tools

Instructions: Think of a time when you were upset. Record what you did to calm yourself. Then expand your thinking to other times and record several more ways you calm yourself. You can also observe how people you work or live with calm themselves.

Ways I calm myself:

Ways other people calm themselves:

Physical tools. When a person is angry or very upset, he may have a restless energy or wish to "do something." Physical activity, particularly involving large muscles, helps a person feel calmer. Running, dancing, and swimming all use large muscles and reduce restless energy. Some children, particularly active kids, need to move in order to calm down.

Caution: Short, quick movements, like hitting a pillow or punching bag, rarely have the same calming effect as large movements. However, hitting a pillow is better than hitting a person. For some kids, hitting a pillow can be used as an intermediate step as they learn other tools. For example, a child might hit a pillow, then shake out his feelings, and eventually calm himself by taking deep breaths.

For some children, movement excites them further. You can help these children by "putting them together." To do that, you put your hands on the sides of their shoulders or hips and firmly press inwards. Over time, these children can learn to put themselves together by wrapping their arms around their shoulders and hugging themselves firmly. (See illustrations on page 116).

Auditory/verbal tools. For some people, crying or screaming when they are upset comes naturally. For many very young children, crying or screaming is their primary way of communicating distress. As children develop language and a feelings vocabulary, they can begin to communicate what they want more clearly.

With some children, simply talking about what upsets them helps them calm down. With others, listening to music may help. Some are calmed by listening to soothing music, others by rousing music that reflects their inner turmoil. Still others prefer starting with dramatic music and gradually changing to soothing music.

Visual tools. Some people calm themselves by detaching from their surroundings and looking outward or inward. Focusing outward they might watch trees sway or read a book. Focusing inward they might go to a calm place in their mind, gently examine what they are feeling, or meditate. Some children can detach in the presence of others and some need to be alone.

Creative. These tools focus the child's energy in a constructive way and usually involve repetitive hand movements. For some people, stringing beads or knitting is soothing. For others, putting their feelings on paper in a picture or in words helps them understand their feelings better and calms them. For creative tools to be effective, the child needs to have some skill so the act of creating does not add more frustration.

Self-comforting tools. Babies are born with a self-soothing skill built in – sucking. Many crying babies are soothed by pacifiers. This oral activity may change to chewing pencils, chewing hair, or smoking cigarettes as kids grow older. However, there are many other ways of self-comforting: getting a hug or back rub, taking a bubble bath, curling up with a good book, lounging outside, drinking a cup of tea, eating a bowl of chicken soup or a piece of chocolate.

Food can help people calm down in two ways. First, when people are hungry, they are often more easily upset. That is why the hour before dinner is so difficult for many families. Eating a nutritious snack can help both parent and children deal with frustration better. Second, even when a person is not hungry, carbohydrates may help because they increase the serotonin level in the brain, which enhances a person's mood.

Although some parents object to children using food for comfort, many of these parents use food to calm themselves or reduce boredom. If you use food for self-calming, you might model eating a piece of fruit, drinking a cup of tea with honey, or even sipping a bowl of soup.

Humor tools. Laughter is a wonderful stress reducer. It has been shown to aid recovery from illness, reduce pain, and generally help people feel better. However, for many people it is a difficult tool to use because humor is highly individual, and few of us were taught how to make light of things.

One way to introduce laughter is with videos and humor books. You can ask a librarian or store clerk for ideas to suit you.

Self-calming strategies

Physical	Stomp, run, swim, dance, bike, knead bread, weed a garden, plant flowers, clean room, organize a closet
Auditory/ verbal	Cry, talk to a friend, listen to music, self-talk (e.g., "Things will get better," or "I've done this before.")
Visual	Visualize yourself in a calm place, read a book, see the uncomfortable feelings floating away, imagine the feelings draining out, watch the trees sway
Creative	Write poetry, write a journal, draw a picture, knit, make models, play the piano, build with Lego's
Self-comforting	Take a bubble bath, ask for a hug, lie down outside, eat chocolate/carbohydrates
Humor	Watch videos, read a humor book, see humor in the situation, make a joke out of it

Another way to use humor is to exaggerate what is upsetting to the point of ridiculousness as seven-year-old Taryn does.

Taryn's best friend, Amy, moved away. Taryn was sad Amy was gone and worried that she wouldn't find another good friend. She spent her time crying and moping about.

One evening while they were cleaning up after supper, she told her mom, "I'm tired of being sad, but I don't know how to stop. And I'm afraid I'll never have another best friend like Amy."

Mom responded that she would probably never have a friend just like Amy, but that she could have a new best friend. When Taryn repeated that she would never, never have another good friend, her mother coached her in humor by exaggerating the situation. "No, you will never, ever, ever have another friend, no matter how old you are. You will live your life in isolation. When someone talks to you at school, you will run away. If she follows, you will hide. And when she finds you, then you . . ."

At this point Taryn broke in and continued the story, "I'll . . . I'll . . . I'll spit in her face to make her go away. And when I'm as old as Grannie, I will board up my windows and put a sign 'Go away' on the door." By this time she was laughing so hard she couldn't talk. When she left the room Mom knew the healing had begun.

Exercise 4-2:
Children's self-calming tools

Instructions: Think about how your child calms down. Check which common strategies your child uses, then add additional tools he or she uses. List additional strategies that might help below.

Common ways children calm themselves.
Check the techniques your child uses to calm himself or herself down.
- ☐ crying
- ☐ asking for a hug
- ☐ stomping his feet
- ☐ sucking a thumb or pacifier

List additional ways your child calms himself or herself.

List three more strategies that might help him or her calm down.

- •
- •
- •

Some children naturally gravitate to seeing humor in situations; others need to be taught. It is usually most effective to begin by modeling humorous exaggeration yourself so the child understands what is happening and doesn't feel that you are making fun of him.

We have looked at six groups of tools. You can find ideas in "Self-calming strategies" above. You can also find descriptions of how some strategies work and how to teach them in Appendix C. "Children's self-calming tools" (Exercise 4-2) focuses on noticing how your child calms herself.

Next we will look at how to introduce coping skills to children.

ℐ How to teach self-calming tools

When children are upset, they need concrete tools to use to calm themselves. Some children develop self-calming techniques on their own. For example, four-year-old Nora found that she could calm herself by curling up in a spot of sun like a cat or wrapping up in a blanket like a hot dog. Her parents helped her make a list of self-calming tools and added a few standards – for example, take a deep breath and march around the house. The list was posted on the refrigerator. If she needed help calming down when she was upset, they would go with her to the refrigerator and remind her she could choose a way to soothe herself.

If your child has effective self-calming tools, fine. If not, you can teach them. However, teaching is very different from telling, as you see below.

Margaret had two children – Neal, age 4, and Megan, age 2. Megan was having major meltdowns several times a day, so Margaret decided to teach both her kids to take a deep breath when they were upset. She chose to start with breathing because her son's gymnastic teacher was talking to the class about the importance of breathing correctly when they did gymnastics. She sat her children down on the sofa and explained that when they were upset they could take deep breaths to calm themselves.

Neal quickly picked up the concept and began to "blow out" his frustration when he was upset. However, Mom's explanation had no impact on Megan. Margaret was tempted to conclude that Megan was too young to learn. However, she wondered if the difference might be that it was easier for Neal because he already knew about breathing and Megan did not.

Teaching kids to deal with feelings is different from telling them what to do. Teaching involves introducing the skill, linking the skill to the feeling of calmness, practicing the skill in pretend, then reminding the child that he has a choice when he is upset. The last step involves backing out and letting the child remember that he has choices himself. We will look at each of these steps.

Introduce the tool. Introducing the tool involves more than saying, "When you are upset take a deep breath." The child needs to practice using the tool while he is calm and life is pleasant.

For example, if your son Adam loves to sit under a tree in the shade, you could teach him to save the calmness he feels in his mind and go there when he was upset. You could begin by sitting with Adam under a tree in the shade and talking about how the sunlight filters through the leaves, the sounds that he hears, and the way the breeze feels on his skin.

Link tool to feeling calm. When the child becomes successful with the action of the tool, then you can link the tool to the feeling of calmness. In this example, you can sit with your son and remark, "My, how pleasant it feels to sit here. I feel calm all over. I'm going to soak up this calmness so I can use it when I need it." Or, sometime when things are going well, you could say, "Adam, let's sit here and go to the calm place." Your purpose is to associate the tool with a feeling of calmness and well-being.

Practice using the tool. When your child can associate calmness with the technique, practice using the tool in pretend. For example, you could say, "Adam, remember this morning when Brian was mean and you started crying? I'm going to pretend Brian is being mean to me, and I'll try to stay calm by going to the calm place in my mind." After you modeled the tool, you can invite Adam to practice going to the calm place in his mind.

You can practice using the calming technique in three ways. One way is strictly pretend. Make up a story and act it out. Another approach is for the child to act out a situation that he or she has experienced, and use the calming tool. This approach may be difficult for some children. At those times, the parent can act out a situation with the child watching. In this way the parent models for the child how the child could use the tool.

Prompt the child to use the tool. Once the child can use a tool in pretend, you can prompt her when she is upset. It is often helpful to phrase the prompt as a choice. "Would you like to take deep breaths or go to a calm place in your mind?" It also helps to offer the choice before the child has totally lost control.

Back out and let a child cope. When your child can choose to calm himself or herself when prompted, it is time to back out and let your child remember without prompting. We can see how this process works by returning to the story of Margaret and her toddler.

Margaret decided to try teaching Megan to take deep breaths. So she invented a breathing game – "Tissue Hockey" – where they blew balls of tissue across the table. When Megan could blow the "ball" across the table, Margaret observed how calm she herself felt inside each time they played.

When Megan could take deep breaths, Margaret started another game. In this game Margaret was Mommy Bear, and when Mommy Bear was upset about something she would take "Big Bear Breaths" to calm herself. Then Margaret asked Megan to pretend to be Bonnie Bear and take a "Bear Breath" when she dropped her fish dinner on the ground. Margaret changed the story several times to give Megan practice.

Once Megan associated taking a breath with getting calm, Margaret began to offer her the choice of crying or taking "Big Bear Breaths." Teaching Megan to take deep breaths was so successful that Margaret decided to teach Megan to "shake out" her feelings. Then Mom was able to offer Megan two choices, "Do you want to shake out the feelings or take a Bear Breath?"

Once Megan could calm herself when prompted, Margaret slowly began to reduce her prompting. Eventually Megan could calm herself without prompting.

In this example, Margaret was successful teaching Megan to calm herself by breaking the task into small pieces. It is important to notice that Margaret let Megan become comfortable taking calming breaths before she asked Megan to use the tool when she was upset. Although parents are often motivated to teach when kids are upset, that is not usually a good time for children to learn. It is helpful to notice that as Megan mastered one stage, Margaret moved on to another level.

You can practice planning how to teach a calming tool in Exercise 4-3. Next we will look at four levels of support parents can offer their children.

ᕒᕐ *Four levels of support for kids' feelings*

There are four ways parents can offer children support – as comforter, teacher, coach, or consultant. This support can be expressed as helping kids calm themselves, solving problems, or teaching basic skills. Each level is appropriate at different times as the child grows. We will look at each level in relation to helping a child calm down after he hears a loud barking dog.

Parent as comforter. This is a role that comes naturally to most parents of infants and toddlers – they provide the comfort for the child. For example, when the baby cries, Dad might pick him up and murmur, "You are okay. I'm here to keep you safe."

It is helpful when parents provide comfort in different ways and explain what they are doing. One time they could offer a hug, another time a song, and a third time gentle rocking. In this way, children can experience different ways to soothe themselves.

Parent as teacher. At this level the parent offers the child choices of how he can calm himself. Ideally these will be ways the child has experienced and understands. For example, the parent might offer, "That dog scared you, but he can't hurt you because he's behind a fence. Would you like to hold my hand or would you like me to pick you up?" Here the parent offers the alternatives but the child makes the choice.

Parent as coach. When a parent coaches a child, the parent provides the structure for the child rather than offering a choice. For example, the parent might say, "Boy, that dog is loud. He's kind of scary even though he's behind the fence. How do you want to calm yourself?" If the child can't think of a way, you can ask him how he calmed himself in a different situation.

Parent as consultant. At the consultant stage, a parent offers support without offering ideas or asking questions. The purpose is to let the child know he can solicit your help if desired, without encouraging him to remain dependent on you. You might say, "Wow, that dog is scary. I'm here if you need me."

Each level is appropriate at some times and not at other times. Some parents become comfortable at one stage and do not think to move on. For example, the parent of a toddler or preschooler may continue to com-

Exercise 4-3:
Plan how to teach a calming tool

Instructions: Read the situation below. Use the five steps to plan what you might say to teach Ronnie to calm himself by running.

Situation: Ronnie, age 4, is an active boy. He is always moving. Mom has noticed that the day goes better when he gets lots of exercise, so she wants to teach him to jog.

1. Introduce the calming tool	
2. Link the tool to feeling calm	
3. Practice using the tool while calm	
4. Prompt child to use the tool	
5. Back out and let child cope	

Possible answers: 1. *Introduce the calming tool:* Go running with Ronnie each evening before supper. 2. *Link the tool to feeling calm:* When finished running, comment that you feel calmer. Next time you run together, ask Ronnie to notice how he feels before and after running. 3. *Practice using the tool while calm:* Let's go running. Remember how upset you were when . . .? Let's pretend you are angry and jog to calm that feeling. 4. *Prompt the child to use the tool:* When he is upset that today's play date is canceled, ask him to go jogging with you. Comment on how calm you feel when you return. Next time he is upset, ask if he wants to jog with you. Continue until he associates jogging with calming himself. 5. *Back out and let the child cope:* When he is upset, remind him that he has a tool to calm himself if he wishes without specifying what it is. Later, let him recall he has a tool himself.

fort a child even when the child is able to learn to comfort himself. When that happens, it is more difficult for the child to learn to calm himself.

On the other hand, even though a person has the skills to calm himself or herself, there are times when comfort is appropriate and appreciated. For example, when a teen or adult has experienced a death or major disappointment, it is often appropriate to offer a hug, a shoulder to cry on, or whatever comfort the person might like.

In this chapter we have looked at six categories of tools a person can use for comforting and four ways parents can support children in their growth. In the next chapter we will look at ways parents can help children solve their own problems.

Chapter Five

Problem-solving tools

A variety of situations upset children. Some involve problems with people, others involve problems with things. Although the process of handling "people" problems is the same as the process of handling "things," some of the techniques for use with people are different.

In this chapter we will look at the process of solving problems, some strategies for dealing with the physical world and with people, how to teach children to negotiate, and stages of support for problem solving. We will begin with looking at the problem-solving process in general.

How to solve a problem

The first step in solving a problem is to stop and focus. Calm yourself and identify what the problem really is. Then generate ideas of what you could do, evaluate those ideas, and make a plan. When you are done, review the plan and how it went. We will look at each of these steps.

Stop and focus. This has two parts: looking at yourself and defining the problem. In order to look at the problem, you need to calm yourself enough to think well. When you are very angry or upset, your body dumps adrenalin into the bloodstream. This helps prepare your body to move boulders or fight lions. However, it inhibits the problem-solving section of the brain, making it more difficult to think clearly. You can use many of the self-soothing techniques described in the previous chapter to calm yourself enough to problem solve.

When you are calm, think about what happened and how you felt, and describe the problem. Sometimes the event that upsets you is not the real problem. For example, one child asked her brother to play catch. He said, "NO" empathically. She was hurt that he would not play with her. Then she asked, "What would you like to play instead?" He said, "Cards. I'm too tired to chase the ball after soccer practice." At first she thought he did not want to play with her, but that was not the problem. He was just too tired to play ball.

Think of ideas. When you have defined the problem, brainstorm. If possible, write your ideas down. Think of as many different ideas as you can. Aim for at least one idea per year of age until twelve. Include silly and crazy ideas. If you have trouble thinking of ideas, you can ask others for suggestions or imagine what a wise person you know might do. If you still have trouble generating ideas, think of what you would do if you had a million dollars or were a magician.

Interestingly, when your mind is free enough to think of silly ideas, it is free enough to think of new, good ideas. At this stage go for quantity; you will sort out what is realistic in the next step. The more ideas you or your child have, the more likely you will be to solve your problem to everyone's satisfaction.

Act effectively. To act effectively you need to evaluate the ideas, select the best one or two, and make a plan to implement them.

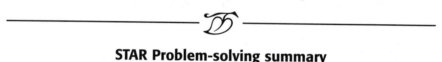

STAR Problem-solving summary

Stop & focus. Stop and calm yourself: notice your feelings, think about why you are upset. Focus on the situation: gather data (what is going on) and identify the problem.

Think of ideas. Think of many ideas – different ideas. Include silly and crazy ones. Write them down. Aim for at least one idea per year of age until twelve.

Act effectively. Evaluate the ideas. Is it realistic and respectful? Does it work both in the immediate and long term? Select the best ideas and make a plan. Choose a time to review how the plan worked.

Review & revise. Review how the plan went. If it worked, consider why it was successful. If it flopped, why did it fail?

When you look at the ideas, consider both the immediate and long-term results. Some ideas can get what you want in the short run, but cause trouble in the long run. For example, when young children dawdle, some parents are tempted to say, "You can come or I'll leave you behind." Since children's greatest fear is abandonment, this often works at the time, however, it introduces a fear of being left that may make it difficult for the child to trust the caregiver and harder for her to form lasting relationships later. Evaluate the ideas. Consider whether each idea is realistic and respectful.

When you have narrowed down the list of ideas, work them into a plan. If you don't have any ideas left after you evaluate all of them, you can brainstorm again or adapt one of the ideas you have.

In planning, consider who, what, when, and where. Who is or should be involved? What resources will you need? When is a good time to start? Where will you do it? It is also helpful to think about how your plan could go wrong and to decide how long you will try this approach before stopping and re-evaluating.

Review and revise. After you try your plan, review how it went – good, ghastly, or somewhere in between. If the idea worked, consider why it was successful. If it did not, consider why it failed. You can use this information the next time you solve a problem.

Sometimes it takes more than one approach to resolve a longstanding problem. So if you are guiding a child through this process, you might ask her what she will do if her chosen approach does not work.

ℐ᧑ *Introduce the problem-solving process*

One of the best ways to teach the problem-solving process is to model using it yourself. In the following example, a serviceman has just phoned to say the missing dryer part will not be in until next week. Mom decided to use this situation to verbalize the problem-solving process for her children.

"I am so angry. The serviceman phoned and said he can't fix the dryer till next week. I don't know what we are going to do. I am so mad. I'll use the STAR problem-solving process.

Calm yourself. *"I need to calm myself so I can think. I'll try blowing out my anger." Blow. Blow. Blow. "Now, I'll check to see if I'm still upset." Pause. "Yes, I'm still mad. I need to take more breaths." Blow. Blow. Blow. Pause to check feelings again. "I'm calmer now."*

Stop and focus. *"Now what is the problem? It seems like I have two problems – nothing clean left to wear and a big mess on the bathroom floor from the overflowing laundry basket. Well, I can ignore the mess for a couple of days. So I'll concentrate on what to wear tomorrow.*

Think. *"I need ideas. Let's see, we can wear dirty clothes. We can buy new clothes. I can borrow clothes from my sister. I can wash clothes and hang them out to dry. If I had a housekeeper, I could send her to the laundromat to wash and dry the clothes."*

Act. *"Next I'll evaluate the ideas, choose one, and make a plan. Okay, I don't want to wear dirty underwear, and I can't afford to buy new clothes for everyone. My sister and her family are out of town, so I can't ask her. I can wash the clothes and hang them on things to dry but that will be messy. And*

I don't have a housekeeper to send to the laundromat. I could go myself, but it would take hours to wash and dry all the clothes. Hmmm. What can I do?

Well, I can collect all the underwear and wash it. Then I can sort through the other clothes and see which are wearable. I can wash a load of outer clothes and then take both loads to the laundromat to dry.

Review. *"When I get done, I can decide how it went."*

This process of problem solving can be used for problems with "people" or "things." The main difference between "people" and "thing" problems will be the type of ideas that you generate. We will look at strategies for both of these.

☙ Strageties to deal with things

Young children are just learning how the physical world works. They may have trouble stacking blocks, pouring water in a glass, untangling a pull toy, or making a marking pen go exactly where they want. This often leads to frustration or crying.

Older children too have trouble making the physical world comply with their wishes – kicking a soccer ball to someone running, playing a musical instrument, winning a computer game, or folding intricate origami.

These situations fall into two classes: lack of understanding of how the world works and lack of skill or ability to do the activity. We will look at each of these.

Lack of understanding. You might think that if the child doesn't understand why his block tower keeps falling down that the best thing would be to simply tell him that the rug is wrinkled and the blocks are unstable. While that is the quickest way to give information, it may not be the most effective way for the child to learn the information.

Usually children learn best discovering things themselves. In this case, you might build two towers, one on a wrinkle and one on a smooth part of the rug. You could observe, "Look! That tower is stable and this one is not. I wonder what the difference is. Why do you think those blocks keep falling down?" If the child doesn't know, you could continue, "What is different? Do you think it could be the wrinkle in the rug?" If the child still doesn't know, then you might add, "Let's build a tower on this wrinkle and see if it is stable."

When the child understands that the wrinkle makes the tower unstable, you can ask, "Where do you think the tower will be stable?" He might suggest the wooden floor, a smooth rug, or a book on the rug.

Helping a child discover the solution definitely takes longer than saying, "Build it here." However, letting the child discover the solution teaches the child to think about the problem: define the problem, generate alternatives and, if you want, even test ideas. Your child learns a process that can be used in many situations.

Lack of skill. Sometimes children get upset because they cannot make the physical world work the way they want it to. For example, if a child wants to play the piano or shoot baskets, he needs to learn how, and that takes time and practice. Many children get frustrated quickly because they can't see progress.

Seven ways to stay focused while you learn are listed below. We can see how they could work if Dylan wants to learn to shoot baskets.

Get a teacher or mentor. Find a person who knows the skill or one who also has experience teaching the skill. This will make it easier to learn and help you avoid common problems. For example, Dylan could ask his neighbor to show him how to shoot baskets, or he could register for summer basketball camp.

Divide the task into small pieces. Take little steps so the task is not overwhelming. For example, Dylan could plan to: (1) Hit the backboard with the ball. (2) Get the ball in the basket for the first time. (3) Sink one ball in every ten tries. (4) Sink one ball in five tries. (5) Sink one in three tries. (6) Start the process again for shooting from another position.

Make practice fun. People find it easier to keep practicing when it is enjoyable. Dylan could make practicing fun by shooting baskets with a friend or rewarding himself for every 50 or 100 baskets he tries.

Chart your progress. Find some way to record your effort or your success. Dylan could put a star on the calendar for each basket he makes. Over time he could see the number of baskets he makes each week increase and recognize his progress.

Take breaks. Whenever you find yourself getting upset, take a break and calm yourself. For example, Dylan might decide to take a "water break" when he starts getting frustrated. You can find many such tools to help children calm down in the previous chapter on calming techniques.

Make a commitment. Sometimes it helps to make a commitment to someone. The commitment may be in terms of "effort" or "results." Effort might be, "I will shoot the ball 50 times every day this week." Results could be, "I will make five baskets every day this week, no matter how many tries it takes."

Imagine yourself as successful. Put lots of detail in your imagination – what you see, hear, feel, etc. Dylan might think, "I can feel the sun on my face as I turn toward the basket. I feel my muscles contract as I lift the ball and toss it toward the basket. It hits the backboard and drops in. I can feel my heart accelerate with excitement. I hear Tony congratulate me. I feel so excited."

Exercise 5-1:
Strategies to deal with things

Instructions: Use the seven tools below to find different strategies for Alice to offer Ian who is upset that he can't play "Twinkle, Twinkle, Little Star" on the trumpet he got two days ago.

Get a teacher or mentor

Divide the task into small pieces

Make practice fun

Chart progress

Take breaks

Make a commitment

Imagine yourself as successful

Possible answers. *Get a teacher:* Sign up for music lessons. *Divide the task:* Divide the page of music into four parts. Practice each separately. *Make practice fun:* Every ten minutes Ian practices he gets a five-minute TV ticket he can use on the weekend. *Chart progress.* Record on a calendar each day how long it takes to play the song correctly (or the number of errors made). You should be able to notice improvement after several days. *Take a break:* Practice 5 minutes, then take 10 deep breaths. Do this every 5 minutes. *Make a commitment:* Practice 15 minutes a day. (Or, agree to play the piece at a family gathering in three weeks.) *Imagine success:* Imagine yourself standing in front of the smiling audience. Each note is clear. The playing is smooth and even. At the end people clap their hands and ask you to play it again.

These strategies can be used for any skill a child wants to learn. You can teach these seven strategies by using them and talking about when you learn something or by musing aloud about how each might work in a situation you face. You could even ask your child to predict what might happen if you used one or two of the strategies.

ℒ♥ *Strategies to deal with people*

Some of children's conflicts are the inevitable result of clashing individual needs and wishes; other conflicts are the result of teasing or malicious intent. We will look at some strategies children can use to deal with other people. However, bullying at any age is a problem in need of grown-up help. Bullying happens only in settings (home or school) where the adults ignore it or accept it as normal behavior. For resources on dealing with bullying, see Appendix E.

The following are ten ways a child can respond to other children. Each is appropriate in some situations and not in others. We will look at how Helen might use them when Paul snatches her hat on the playground before school.

Clarify the situation. A child clarifies the situation and states her expectations. This should be done in a clear, firm tone. Helen might say, "That is my hat. Please give it to me." This tool can also be used to collect information. The questions need to be asked in a friendly, curious manner. For example, "Paul, you have snatched my hat every day this week. What is so compelling about my hat?"

Negotiate differences. To negotiate the child needs to find out what the other person wants, and talk about ways both their needs can be met. This process will be discussed more in the section on "How to help children negotiate."

Ignore the problem. Children are often advised to ignore teasing and obnoxious behavior, but this is a difficult tool to use. Ignoring can be effective when the other child wants to get attention, but only if everyone ignores him. That is because sometimes the teasing occurs in order to get the bystanders' response as well the victim's. In this case, Helen and her friends would continue talking or playing as though Paul were invisible and nothing had happened.

Reframe the situation. To see the problem a new way, the child finds a positive element in the problem or finds a way to discount the negative element so the problem no longer upsets him or her. In this case, Helen might think, "Paul's my friend. I know he will return my hat. I'll let him play with it now if he wants to."

Change or move. This involves going to a safe or protected place. Helen might decide to go directly into school, rather than playing in the schoolyard.

Distract or divert. Distracting involves doing something in a way that draws the other child's attention. The distraction can be something you say or do. Helen might tap her friend on the shoulder while pointing to the sky and say, "Look at that!" If her friend looks where she is pointing, Paul will probably look too. While Paul is looking, Helen might grab her hat back.

Use humor. One way to find humor in a situation is to exaggerate the situation to the point of ridiculousness. For example, Helen might imagine that she has a magic hat. And every time Paul snatched it off another hat would instantly appear. She could imagine Paul's frustration as he was surrounded waist high in hats. When you can smile at an image in your mind it helps you maintain control of your feelings and deal with the situation.

Do something unexpected. Something unexpected can be giving the other child exactly what he wanted or preventing it in an unexpected way. Helen might sew a strap on her hat so that when Paul tries to snatch her hat it would not come off, or she could bring lots of hats. When Paul snatches her hat, Helen and her friend could say, "Oh, Paul wants a hat, here is another," and toss them to him one at a time.

Get help. When a child has tried unsuccessfully to handle a situation, it is appropriate for the child to get help. The help can be from a friend or an adult. In this case after asking for her hat back, Helen could go to the playground supervisor and ask for help.

One way to help a child understand the difference between "telling" and "tattling" is to read the book *Telling Isn't Tattling* by Kathryn Hammerseng.

Use force. Another option children have is to solve the problem with force. In this situation, Helen would try to grab her hat back.

These alternatives are presented in *Heidi's Irresistible Hat,* a book in the children's series "Kids Can Choose." This and other books in the series are listed in Appendix E. You can practice using these tools in Exercise 5-2: Strategies to deal with people. Next we will look at how to help children resolve problems by themselves through negotiation.

ᴇ♥ *Help children negotiate*

The ability to negotiate is an excellent skill. The negotiation process is very similar to the problem-solving process. However, before children can learn to negotiate, they need three skills.

Prerequisite skills. First, children need the ability to listen and pay attention. It is impossible to negotiate if you do not understand what the other person wants. Second, children need some basic language con-

Exercise 5-2:
Strategies to deal with people

Instructions: Use the ten tools below to find ways that Diane might respond when her friend Jessica says, "That is the ugliest dress I have ever seen." Remember, some strategies sound strange or may be unsuitable.

Clarify the situation: Distract or divert:

Ignore the problem: Do something unexpected:

Re-frame the situation: Use humor:

Negotiate differences: Get help.

Change or move: Use force.

Possible answers: Clarify the situation: Ask, "What is wrong with this dress?" *Ignore:* Do not respond to the comment. *Re-frame the situation:* Decide Jessica must be jealous of the new dress. *Negotiate differences:* Respond, "You don't like my dress. I do like it. What can we do so we can both be happy? *Change or move:* Move so you can't hear Jessica's comments. *Distract or divert:* Say, "Speaking of ugly dresses, did you see the new issue of *People* magazine?" *Do something unexpected:* Say, "I love to hear you criticize. You do it so well." *Use humor:* "It is hideous, isn't it? My goal was to be the worst dressed person today. I have succeeded!" *Get help:* Ask your mother (or friend) for ways to respond. *Use force:* not appropriate

cepts: same and different, if-then, why-because. These concepts are needed to discuss the ideas presented. Third, children need to understand feelings, as discussed in Chapter 3. When children have these prerequisite skills, you can begin to teach them to negotiate.

Steps to facilitate negotiation. The five steps to teach children to negotiate are a little different from the steps children use by themselves. When you help children learn to negotiate, your role is to help the children find a solution, not to offer ideas or advice yourself.

Step 1. Gather data. When children are upset, you need to find out what is going on. You can ask open-ended questions like: What happened? How did you feel when . . . ? What happened then?

The purpose of the questions is to gather data. Don't be surprised if the children's explanations of what happened differ. All you need to know is enough to identify the problem.

When you know what happened, you can decide if you want to invoke a family rule, offer the children choices, or help them resolve the situation themselves. If you decide to help them negotiate, you can use this process.

Mom helps her sons negotiate after finding them fighting on the floor in the living room.

Mom: Ben and Tom, come sit with me. What happened?

Ben: He took my chair.

Tom: I did not. It was empty.

Ben: I went to get a drink. You knew I was coming back.

Tom: I did not.

Mom intervenes.

Mom: Ben, how was Tom to know you were coming back?

Ben: He knows. I always watch my show in the afternoon.

Mom: Tom, why did you want that chair?

Tom: I want to read and that is the most comfortable chair.

Step 2. State the problem clearly. It is easier for children to negotiate if they know what the problem is. State the problem in terms of both children's needs.

Mom: We have two children who want to sit in the same chair. What can we do so they will both be happy?

It is important to add the "both be happy" because children are egocentric. Both will need to feel satisfied.

Step 3. Generate ideas. Encourage many different ideas. Write the ideas down if you can't remember *all* of them. If you forget an idea, the child who suggested it may conclude you didn't like it. Encourage silly ideas. Aim for at least one idea per year of age until twelve.

When negotiating we separate the process of generating ideas from evaluating them. If a child gets upset about another person's idea, remind him that "Right now we are thinking of ideas. Later we will choose an idea."

Mom: I'm ready to record your ideas.

Ben: Tom can read somewhere else.

Tom: I don't want to read somewhere else.

Mom: Right now we are thinking of ideas. Later you can tell why you don't like that idea.

Tom: I get the chair and Ben tapes the show to see it later.

Ben: No! I had . . .

Mom interrupts: . . . Ben, an idea, please.

Ben: We can buy a new chair so we each have one.

Tom: Ben goes over to Josh's house to watch the show.

Mom: We have five ideas: Ben gets the chair. Tom gets the chair. Ben tapes the show. We buy a new chair. Ben goes next door to watch. What else?

Ben: Tom can use my quilt and sit in the old chair.

Tom: Ben can wrap up in his quilt on the old chair.

Mom: We need some really different ideas.

Ben: I can watch TV now, and he can use the chair when I'm done.

Step 4. Evaluate the ideas. With older children you can go through each idea one by one and ask if it is reasonable, respectful, or realistic. With young children you can ask, "Do you think any ideas will work for both of you?"

Mom: Ben, what idea do you think Tom would like?

Ben: He'd like to sit here now. But I don't want that.

Mom: Tom, what idea do you think Ben would like?

Tom: He would like to watch now and let me use the chair later.

Mom: Would that work for you?

Tom: No. Why should I have to give it up, just to make him happy?

Mom: It looks like none of the ideas work for both of you. Tom, what would make you happy if Ben had the chair?

Tom: He could do something nice for me – like set the table for me or clean my room.

Mom: Ask him if he is willing to do that.

Tom: Ben, are you willing to set the table for me tonight if I let you sit in the chair now?

Ben: Yes. And you can sit in the chair while I set the table.

Step 5. Ask for a decision and help the children plan. When there are several acceptable ideas, list them and ask for a decision. If only one idea is left, ask each child if it is acceptable to him. Then help the kids plan how to implement the decision and choose a time to review how the decision worked. When they have resolved the problem, praise them.

Mom: Tom, is it okay if Ben sits in the chair now and sets the table for you this evening?

Tom: Yes.

Mom: Ben, are you willing to set the table for Tom tonight so you can sit in the chair to watch TV now?

Ben: Yes.

Mom: When should we review this decision?

Tom: (Looking at Ben) How about at dinner?
Ben: Fine.
Mom: Wow, you guys thought of nine ideas and found one that works for
    both of you. I'm impressed.

In this example, Mom kept the boys focused on problem solving and refrained from suggesting ideas. Helping children negotiate is a time-consuming process in the short run, but it saves a great deal of time and emotional energy in the long run, because the children learn to resolve their issues. This process is discussed more fully in the book *Kids Can Cooperate* by Elizabeth Crary.

The job of parents, whether helping children deal with people or things, is to work themselves out of a job. This transition can be seen in the stages of supporting kids' problem solving.

Supporting kids' problem solving

As children grow, parents need to change how they help children solve problems. In the first stage you comfort the child at a very young age (that means solving the child's problem), then teach by offering choices, next coach by providing structure, and finally consult by listening as the child thinks. Let's see how this works when Riley wants to play with the truck his older brother Simon is using.

Parent as comforter. When a baby or young toddler wants something, parents often distract the younger child or ask the older child to let the baby use it. In both of these responses the parent comforts the child by solving the problem.

When parents describe what they are doing and why, the child learns about possible solutions. For example, Dad might say, "Oh, you're upset. You want the fire engine Simon is using. Let's play 'Hide and Seek' while we wait for Simon to finish." Dad labels the tool he is using ("waiting") so that Riley can see it as a tool. It is helpful to use a variety of alternatives. To solve a toy problem, a child can wait, trade for another toy, make a bargain (offer to do sibling's chores if old enough), take turns, or use the toy together. The more alternatives the child has experienced, the easier it will be for him to resolve conflicts on his own.

Parent as teacher. As children grow, they need to take a more active part in their happiness. In this stage the parent offers choices to the child and lets the child decide what to do.

For example, Dad might ask, "You want to play with the fire engine Simon is using. Do you want to wait until Simon's done or find a toy he might like to trade?" Initially this might involve helping the child consider what Simon might like. For example, you might say, "What do you think Simon might like to play with?" If Riley has no idea you could add, "Do you think Simon would prefer to use your aid car or play with your new ball?" Once you have suggested trading two or three times, it is important to back out and let your child think of ideas himself.

Parent as coach. Before children can be effective solving their problems, they need practice thinking of ideas for themselves. As coach, your job is to provide a structure to help children resolve their own problem if they can. The structure can help them define the problem and generate ideas or recall information they have. For example, you might say, "You really want the fire engine Simon has. What are you going to do?" If he says, "I don't know," you can say, "I remember you wanted the police car he was using this morning. What did you do then?" Or, "Remember the story *I Want It*? What did Amy consider doing when she wanted the truck Megan had?" In this way, you are reminding him of the information he already has.

Parent as consultant. In this stage the parent serves as a sounding board for the child's ideas rather than offering ideas or structure. You let the child know you are listening by reflecting back what you hear him or her say. For example, "You're really disappointed that Simon has the fire engine you want. Let me know if you want support." Then drop the subject completely unless he asks for your help.

In this chapter we have looked at how children can deal with disappointment by solving problems with people or things. In the next chapter, we will consider the two elements (feelings and event) together and decide which one to work on first.

Chapter Six

Teaching both feelings and problem solving

Frankie (2 years) is angry because his red crayon broke.

Caitlin (4 years) is crying because the balloon she refused to tie to her wrist has floated away.

Timothy (8 years) comes home from school with shoulders drooping because his friend Eric won't play ball with him.

To most adults, such events are part of living – they happen. We shrug them off. But children often feel events as deliberately hurtful toward them.

When events like these happen in children's lives, parents tend to fix the problem or comfort the child. If we continue the same response as children grow older, we risk encouraging children to be dependent on us to solve all their problems – large and small. Instead, we can teach them to comfort themselves and solve their own problems. For most children learning is a slow process – like learning a foreign language or a complex musical instrument rather than learning to name animals or count to ten.

Most, but not all, of the problems a child faces can be handled by responding to either the "feeling" or the "event." Parents generally focus on one or the other, however, children need help with both.

In this chapter we are going to contrast these ways of responding and consider when you might want to focus on the feeling and when the situation.

✐ *Four ways to respond*

When a child is upset, you can respond to the feeling or to the event that precipitated the feeling. You can also teach the child skills to calm himself or to solve his problems himself.

Focus on the feeling. When a parent responds to the feeling, she tries to soothe or distract the child. She does what she can to stop the distress. Frankie's mother, in the first example, might respond to his feelings. She could get on his level and say, "Oh, no. Your crayon broke. You feel angry. Would you like a hug from Mommy?"

With Caitlin, a parent might respond, "You're sad because your balloon flew away. Wave bye-bye." If she continued to cry, Dad might pull out the pocket watch that intrigues Caitlin and say, "Caitlin, look, here is my watch. Listen. Is it ticking?" In this way he would distract Caitlin from her feelings.

Focus on the event or problem. When a parent responds to the situation, she tries to fix the item or get a new one. Again, she does what she can to reduce the child's distress. A parent focusing on the broken crayon event might reply, "Oh, dear. Your crayon broke. I'll tape it together for you and it will work as good as new." If that did not comfort Frankie, Mom might say, "Hold on. I'll go get you another crayon from my set."

Caitlin's dad might say, "Don't cry. I see the balloon man. We can buy another one."

These two responses are designed to comfort the child. They are the first level of support. There is nothing wrong with this type of support some of the time. However, if it is your only or standard response when your children are upset, they may become dependent on you to make them happy.

Teaching about feelings. The intent here is to give children information when they are calm about comforting themselves, and then remind them of what you have practiced together when they are upset.

With Frankie, Mom might say, "You are really mad that your crayon broke." If she had been reading and singing the book *When You're Mad and You Know It* by Elizabeth Crary (text is in Appendix D), Mom could add, "Do you want to 'blow' or 'shake your feelings out?'" Frankie would be more likely to try the suggestion if they had read and acted out the book together many times. And if Mom began to sing and act the story out after offering him the choice, he would be even more likely to join in.

When Caitlin's balloon floats away, her dad could say, "Oh, your balloon's gone. You look kind of sad to me." If Dad has been talking about feelings, he could add "How do you feel inside? What do you want to do to feel better? Cry, ask for a hug, go for a walk?" In this way he is relating calming tools they have practiced to the current situation.

Teaching problem solving. The goal of teaching problem solving is to give kids the skills they need to resolve their difficulties.

At age two, Frankie is just beginning to develop cause and effect thinking, so teaching him about why his crayon broke will take time and probably involve the destruction of many crayons. However, his mother can demonstrate the process of thinking about the problem.

She might begin, "You are really upset. You were drawing with your red crayon and it broke. You're really angry because you like the red crayon." Mom's voice calms Frankie somewhat, and she continues. "The broken crayon still works. (Mom draws a line.) Is that okay?"

If Frankie says, "Broken," Mom might say, "Oh, the problem is you want a long crayon. Let's think of ways to get a long crayon. What can you do?" Frankie looks at her with a confused expression. "Well, you can ask me to fix this crayon or find another one. What do you want to do?" Frankie points at his broken crayon.

His mother continues, "Oh, you want to fix your crayon. What will we need?" Again he looks confused. "We will need tape. Do you know where the tape is?" He runs to the counter and gets the tape. When he brings the tape back, Mom repairs the crayon.

She sums up, "You were angry that your crayon broke. You calmed down and decided you wanted your crayon fixed. You got the tape and I fixed the crayon. Now you feel content again."

Teaching the problem-solving process takes time. In this example, Mom made some adaptations because Frankie was young. With older children you would wait for their ideas and you would ask them to evaluate the ideas. However, since Mom was introducing the process, she shortened it. Now let's see how this process might work with a somewhat older child.

STAR Problem-solving summary

Stop & focus. Stop and calm yourself. Focus on the situation: gather data and identify the problem.

Think of ideas. Think of lots of ideas, different ideas. Aim for at least one idea per year of age until twelve.

Act effectively. Evaluate the ideas. Decide on a workable idea and make a plan. Choose a time to review the plan.

Review & revise. Review your success. Revise your plan if needed.

When Caitlin was upset, her dad could help her calm down. Later, when she was in a good mood, he might remind her of the situation and ask for her ideas about what she could do differently.

He might begin with, "Remember this morning when your balloon floated away? You were really sad. (Caitlin nodded.) I think it would be fun to play 'Turn the clock back' and think about what you could do differently."

Caitlin, "Okay."

Dad began, "You were sad when the balloon floated away. What happened?"

"The wind pulled it out of my hand," she answered.

Dad wanted to remind her that if she had tied the balloon to her wrist the wind couldn't have pulled it away, but he did not. Instead he asked, "The problem is that the wind pulled your balloon away? Let's think of things to do so next time you have a balloon the wind won't be able to take it away from you. I'll write the ideas down."

"I could wrap the string around and around and around my hand so the wind can't take it away."

Dad replied, "Okay. I wrote that down. What else could you do?"

"I could tie it to a stone, 'cause the wind can't move stones,"

"So you could. What else?" asked Dad.

"You could tie the balloon on my arm. Or, I could tie it on your arm," Caitlin said with a giggle.

Dad summed the ideas up, "You have thought of four ways to keep the balloon from floating away: wrap the string around your hand, tie it to a stone, tie it to your wrist, or tie it to my wrist. Let's consider each one. What might happen if you wrapped the string around your hand?"

"It would stay."

"What about the stone?

"I might get tired carrying the stone."

"How would tying it to my wrist or yours work?" Dad asked.

"Not good to tie it to yours, 'cause then it would be your balloon, not mine. When you tie it to my wrist, it's too tight."

"So what is the best idea, Caitlin?"

"I don't know. Maybe tie it on my hand. Oh, I know."

"What's that?" Dad asked.

"Maybe it wouldn't hurt if you tied it loose."

"Now we have five ideas. So if we turned the clock back, is that what you would do?" Dad asked.

"Maybe," she replied.

"Well, next time you get a balloon you can recall the ideas and try another one. Then decide if you like that idea."

Again, the process takes time; however, it teaches basic thinking skills that are useful in many situations. It is a bit like teaching math facts, you have to practice and practice and then eventually kids remember to use the facts by themselves.

We have looked at what it would be like to comfort the child or solve the problem for the child. We have also discussed how to teach your child to comfort herself or resolve her problem herself.

e~ *A challenge -"You're not my best friend"*

Let's take another look at the different ways to respond to events in kids' lives. In this example, Timothy's mother realizes that she has to deal with the moment and also do some long-term training.

Timothy is a sensitive child. He is tuned into his feelings and those of others. One day last month he came home from school with his shoulders drooping and a very long face. When I asked what was wrong, he said that Eric (his best friend) would not play ball with him.

He looked so sad my heart went out to him. I know he has had trouble dealing with unhappiness and sometimes takes things personally even when they aren't meant that way. So I wondered how to respond. He needs skills to keep from getting so despondent and to cope with the situation rather than becoming a target for teasing.

At the moment, I acknowledged his feelings and offered comfort. "You look really sad. I'd feel sad if my best friend didn't want to be with me. Would you like a hug or would you like to make cookies with me?" Timothy brightened considerably and said, "Both." So I gave him a hug and we made chocolate chip cookies.

Later, as I thought about the situation, I decided I needed to do something because his troubles with friends were getting more frequent. So I divided a paper into quarters and made four lists: What Timothy might feel like; what he could do about his feelings; what the problem was; and what he might do about the situation.

Possible feelings	*Possible problems*
• Hurt or left out	• Eric does not want to play now.
• Angry	• Eric wants power over Timothy.

Ways to deal with feeling	*Ways to respond to the situation*
• Tell Eric how he feels.	• Say, "Okay, when you want to play ball, call me."
• Cry.	• Say, "Okay, I'll see you later."
• Take a deep breath.	• Ask Eric, "What would you like to play?"
• Rub the "magic" stone he carries in his pocket.	• Find someone else to play with now
• Draw a picture of how he feels.	• Start spending more time with other friends
• Rock himself in the rocker when he gets home.	

I decided that Eric probably meant to upset Timothy, so I would teach Timothy to remain calm and to respond to Eric in a neutral way.

To help him calm down, I decided to work on things he could do at school: Take a deep breath, rub his magic stone, and imagine himself being filled with calm. I would teach him how to calm himself (see Chapter 4). After he could calm himself down, we would move onto dealing with the situation.

I decided to use puppets to help him practice options in the situation. He has a favorite stuffed animal we call "Wise Owl." I thought that if Willy the puppet had a problem and asked Wise Owl for advice, Timothy might pay more attention to Wise Owl's advice than to what I suggested.

The first time, I played both Willy and Wise Owl. Then I asked Timothy to play Willy since it is hard for me to use two puppets. Later he wanted to play Wise Owl. That was fine. I brought in another puppet, Wanda the Witch, who got in trouble for turning people who upset her into toads. Timothy, through the Wise Owl puppet, was able to help Wanda think of other ways to deal with her problem.

The last thing I did was to ask Timothy one day, "Do you think Wise Owl could help you deal with Eric?" He got a grin on his face and nodded.

The whole process, calming down and learning ways to respond to Eric, took several weeks of working almost every day, but we were successful in the end.

In this example, Mom worked on both calming tools and people skills. She started with the skills Timothy had and added new skills. A script for a Wise Owl skit is in Appendix D. You can practice distinguishing between the feeling and the situation in Exercise 6-1.

✐ Is teaching skills worth the effort?

Teaching kids to problem solve takes time. Some parents wonder, "Is it really worth the effort?" That depends. First, if you want a child who can make her own happiness by comforting herself and solving her problems, then this will help her learn what she needs to know.

Second, parents and teachers who deliberately teach their children to negotiate and resolve problems report that after the first three months children, even preschoolers, can usually resolve their quarrels. In the long term, this is a huge savings in time and emotional energy for everyone.

✐ Where should I start?

To figure out whether to start with calming skills or problem-solving skills, first identify the skills your child has, next look at how you nor-

Exercise 6-1:
Identifying feelings and events

Instructions: Read each situation. Identify what the child might be feeling. Then identify the event that has upset the child.

Situation	Feeling	Event
Adam (18 months) is hitting you because he can't use the marking pens on the sofa.		
Brenda (24 months) is sobbing because the blossoms are falling off the cherry tree out front.		
Charles (30 months) is lying on the floor flailing because you won't let him cut with a sharp knife.		
Daniel (4 years) is sobbing because his best friend just said to him, "You're not my friend anymore."		
Ellie (5 years) is heartbroken that her best friend has moved away.		
Fiona (6 years) is throwing things at Mom because she cannot watch TV before she's ready for school.		
Greg (7 years) is moping around the house because he can't play soccer as well as his older brother.		
Hanna (8 years) is accusing everyone of taking the red bead necklace that she cannot find.		
Ivan (9 years) is bemoaning the stupidity of the world that let his friends go to soccer camp and not him.		

continued on page 62

Situation	Feeling	Event
Jessica (10 years) is crushed that she did not get the part of princess in the class play.		
Kathy (11 years) is hurt that Sara, her best friend, said her shoes were stupid.		
Lyon (12 years) is incensed that his teacher gave him a "C" on a paper even though he threw it together at the last minute.		

Possible answers: *Adam:* mad, wants to mark on sofa. *Brenda:* disappointed, blossoms are falling from the tree. *Charles:* furious, wants to cut with a knife. *Daniel:* hurt, friend's rejection. *Ellie:* sad, friend is gone. *Fiona:* livid, wants to watch TV now! *Greg:* depressed, can't pass the soccer ball. *Hanna:* scared, necklace is lost. *Ivan:* left out, can't go to camp with friends. *Jessica:* unappreciated, did not get part in play. *Kathy:* hurt/rejected, friend criticized her shoes. *Lyon:* angry/embarrassed, got a low grade on paper

mally respond to your child's distress, then decide on what you want to teach.

Identify needed skills. Using the "Feelings skills inventory" in Exercise 6-2, check the skills your child has. Then list the skills you want your child to learn. Focus on the two or three skills you think he needs most because it is easier to remember one or two things at a time. As he learns those skills, you can add more.

Notice how you respond. When your child is upset, do you do more comforting or teaching him skills? Or do you do both about equally? Do you focus on the feelings or do you fix the situation? Think about the last time your child was upset and recall what you did.

Decide where to start. When you have decided what your child needs and noticed what you do, where to start will probably become clearer. For example, if you usually comfort or distract your preschooler when he is upset, you may want to begin to teach him to comfort himself. Or, if you always fix things for your school-age daughter, you may want to start teaching her to solve her problems.

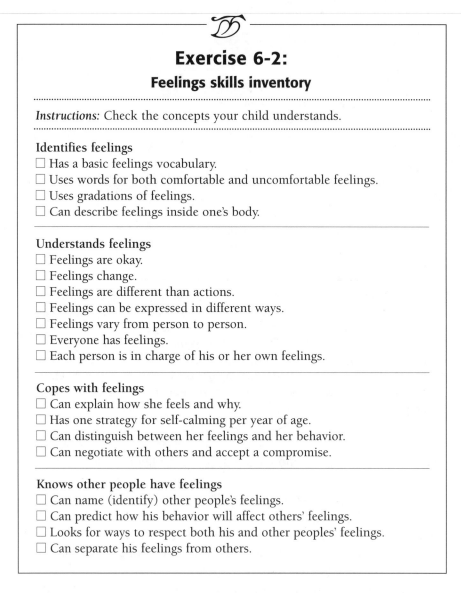

Exercise 6-2:
Feelings skills inventory

Instructions: Check the concepts your child understands.

Identifies feelings
☐ Has a basic feelings vocabulary.
☐ Uses words for both comfortable and uncomfortable feelings.
☐ Uses gradations of feelings.
☐ Can describe feelings inside one's body.

Understands feelings
☐ Feelings are okay.
☐ Feelings change.
☐ Feelings are different than actions.
☐ Feelings can be expressed in different ways.
☐ Feelings vary from person to person.
☐ Everyone has feelings.
☐ Each person is in charge of his or her own feelings.

Copes with feelings
☐ Can explain how she feels and why.
☐ Has one strategy for self-calming per year of age.
☐ Can distinguish between her feelings and her behavior.
☐ Can negotiate with others and accept a compromise.

Knows other people have feelings
☐ Can name (identify) other people's feelings.
☐ Can predict how his behavior will affect others' feelings.
☐ Looks for ways to respect both his and other peoples' feelings.
☐ Can separate his feelings from others.

☙ When should I start?

Start today! Some parents think, or hope, that their children will learn to deal with their feelings themselves. That rarely happens. If your child is younger than three, she is still learning about feelings. You can make it easier for her and for yourself by offering her vocabulary, activities, and structure that make learning more enjoyable. If your child is older than four and still gets upset whenever he does not get what he wants, he probably needs your help learning how to manage his feelings. In either case, you can begin today.

Remember that the best time to teach your child coping strategies is while he is calm. When your child is upset, his mind is awash in feelings and cannot use the information he has or take in new information. Even adults experience this, as illustrated in the story below.

Last year my great uncle was visiting me. One afternoon he had a stroke. I rushed to call 911. When they asked me for my address I couldn't remember it – even though I had lived in the house for five years. Fortunately, I had posted it above the phone the way most fire departments recommend. I am still amazed that I could not remember something so basic.

You can incorporate "feeling learning" into your everyday activities. For example, before you read a book to a child you can look at the pictures with her and ask: "How does _____ (the character) feel?" "Why might she feel that way?" "What can she do to feel better?" Or, if you are watching a video with your son, you could stop it when something happens and ask, "How do you think she felt when he said that?" or "What can she do about that situation?" In these ways you can begin teaching skills today in preparation for tomorrow's challenges.

In this chapter we have looked at the two elements of teaching feelings – skills to calm or soothe oneself and skills to solve problems. You can practice identifying different responses in Exercise 6-3 on page 66. Once you have decided how you respond and what you want to teach your child, it is helpful to make an overall plan for how to proceed. We will discuss that in the next chapter.

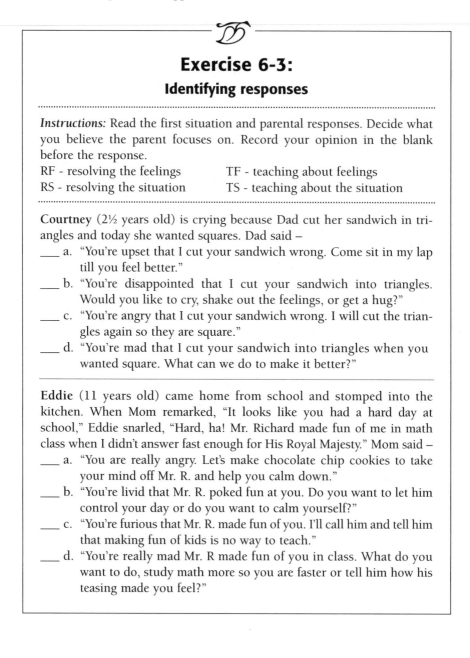

Exercise 6-3:
Identifying responses

Instructions: Read the first situation and parental responses. Decide what you believe the parent focuses on. Record your opinion in the blank before the response.

RF - resolving the feelings   TF - teaching about feelings
RS - resolving the situation   TS - teaching about the situation

Courtney (2½ years old) is crying because Dad cut her sandwich in triangles and today she wanted squares. Dad said –

___ a. "You're upset that I cut your sandwich wrong. Come sit in my lap till you feel better."

___ b. "You're disappointed that I cut your sandwich into triangles. Would you like to cry, shake out the feelings, or get a hug?"

___ c. "You're angry that I cut your sandwich wrong. I will cut the triangles again so they are square."

___ d. "You're mad that I cut your sandwich into triangles when you wanted square. What can we do to make it better?"

Eddie (11 years old) came home from school and stomped into the kitchen. When Mom remarked, "It looks like you had a hard day at school," Eddie snarled, "Hard, ha! Mr. Richard made fun of me in math class when I didn't answer fast enough for His Royal Majesty." Mom said –

___ a. "You are really angry. Let's make chocolate chip cookies to take your mind off Mr. R. and help you calm down."

___ b. "You're livid that Mr. R. poked fun at you. Do you want to let him control your day or do you want to calm yourself?"

___ c. "You're furious that Mr. R. made fun of you. I'll call him and tell him that making fun of kids is no way to teach."

___ d. "You're really mad Mr. R made fun of you in class. What do you want to do, study math more so you are faster or tell him how his teasing made you feel?"

Chapter Seven

Making changes

Many parents who would like to teach their children to calm themselves or deal with their problems find the task daunting. This may be either because they were not taught to understand or cope with their own feelings or because their child's feelings are so intense that parents don't know what to do. We will approach this in two ways. First we will look at ways to introduce general feelings skills. Then we will look at how to teach the specific skills a child needs.

ℐ❧ *Introducing general skills*

As we have discussed in the previous chapters, children need to develop a feelings vocabulary, understand the nature of feelings, discover self-calming strategies, and learn how to resolve their problems. This information can be introduced as you go through your daily routines with children.

Expand your language. Most parents find it relatively easy to incorporate names of colors, animals, actions, and places in their conversation. With a young child they might say, "Look, there's a black dog. He's running across the grass," "Wow, the Tyrannosaurus rex is really big," or while watching a Mariners' baseball game, "Ichiro is from Japan. Let's get the map and see where that is."

Similarly, you can include information about feelings in your everyday conversations. "I'll bet the black dog feels playful. Look at how he's jumping around." "The dinosaur is really large. How would you feel if you saw him in the park?" "Ichiro hit another home run. He must feel proud."

One way to introduce feelings words into your conversation is to pick a "feeling word of the day or week" and look for ways to use it in your conversation. If you have trouble deciding on a word, pick a number between 1 and 20 and use the word from the "Basic feelings vocabulary" below. Or, if you are feeling more adventuresome, choose a word from "101 Feelings words" on page 24. After you choose a word, look within yourself or around you for examples of that feeling and find ways to work the word into your conversation with children.

Basic feelings vocabulary

1. confident / strong	8. excited	15. restless / bored
2. confused	9. frustrated	16. sad
3. content / relaxed	10. happy	17. scared
4. curious	11. lonely	18. silly / goofy
5. disappointed	12. mad / angry	19. tired
6. elated	13. misunderstood	20. worried / anxious
7. embarrassed	14. proud	

Use family routines and rituals. You can talk about feelings during your family activities.

Departures, returns, and transitions. You (or your child) can make a "feelings dial" from a paper plate (see Appendix B) and post it inside your front door. When your child leaves home, he can point the arrow to how he feels. When he returns, he can move the arrow to his current feeling. This will help him identify his feelings and notice that feelings change.

If your child is worried, angry, or upset about something, you now have the opportunity to discuss why your child feels that way and what he can do about his feelings or the situation.

Mealtime. You can incorporate your "feeling word of the day" into conversation during meals. You can recall a situation from work or a story from your youth. Another way to do this is to pick the word at the table and ask each person to talk about a time when he or she felt that way. It helps the process along if a parent begins by sharing his or her experience first.

You can also introduce feelings into conversation by sharing the high and low point of the day. These points can be moderate or dramatic as the events of the day dictate. For example, if you were taking a night class you might share, "The high point was getting a 94 on the math test, and the low point was when Mr. Smith called on me and I could not think of the answer."

You could then elaborate about these events and discuss the feelings and the event, for example, "I'm proud of getting a 94 in math. I'm going to frame the test and put it on my desk to remind me that hard work pays off. I was really embarrassed when I didn't know the answer to the question Mr. Smith asked. I wanted to crawl in a hole and disappear. I had to take calming breaths so I could listen to the rest of class."

With older children you can use high/low points, described above, or choose a feeling word from a deck of feelings cards. You can make a deck by writing words on 3x5 cards or by purchasing the *Feeling Elf Cards* referenced in Appendix E. Again, children can discuss the event, the feelings, what the child did, and options for the future. When you listen to your child's experience, maintain an attitude of mild interest. If you act bored, he may not continue. If you are very interested, he may withhold comments and create a power struggle. Remember that whenever you start the routine, you may need to model sharing your experiences several times before your children are willing to share theirs.

Homework. You can incorporate feelings talk into doing homework. Using a "feelings dial" or other system, you can talk with your child about how he feels when he begins and ends an assignment. If your child looks frustrated, you can remark, "That math must be hard. You look really frustrated." When he is done you could reflect, "You look relieved to have finished your math."

If your child is having a lot of trouble, you could say, "Looks like you are really upset. It's hard to learn when your mind is upset. What can you do to calm yourself so the work will be easier?" Using homework as a springboard for understanding feelings is illustrated in the following example.

Jean's fourth-grade daughter, Christa, was having a great deal of trouble writing a report for history. Christa didn't like history and she didn't have experience writing such a complex report. Past experience suggested that Christa would probably be very emotional during the several days it would take to complete the project.

Jean agreed to help her and added they would first make a written plan for writing the report (dealing with the situation) and also take a break every twenty minutes to share their feelings. They assigned a value of 1 to 10 for how upset they were. When Christa was upset Jean helped her calm down, by taking a break, eating a snack, or imagining herself in a calm place. Jean also helped Christa notice what helped her feel calmer.

What surprised Jean most was that the way they felt at any given time could be quite different. Christa might be upset and Jean fine. Once, Jean was very frustrated, a nine on their scale, and Christa was only a two. Until they shared their numbers, Jean assumed they both were equally frustrated at the same time.

In this situation, Christa was learning four things at once: how to write a report, how to tune into her feelings, how to calm herself, and that people can have different feelings about the same thing.

Bedtime rituals. Bedtime is a natural time to reflect on the experiences of the day, to savor the pleasant experiences, and to let go of the unpleasant ones. Reflect on the day. Ask what happened. Ask your child how she felt. Ask open-ended questions so your child will have the opportunity to say more than yes or no.

Many young children respond to feeling faces drawn on your fingertips. You can make these faces into happy, sad, mad, and scared *feeling finger puppets.* Then you can ask, "Which face did you feel like today?" If the feeling is pleasant, you can ask if that is a feeling he or she wants to remember. If the answer is yes, you can make a point to review the feeling now or enter the event in a notebook on feelings.

You may wish to encourage older children to keep a journal, writing a bit each day about what happened, how they felt, and what they did. Journaling can be a way to savor pleasant experiences and let go of unpleasant ones. For many older children reading their journals can help them notice recurring themes and encourage them to find new ways to deal with the situations.

Each of these activities can be used to reflect on feelings and how you or your child responds to them.

Expand story time. When you are reading a picture book, you can look at the pictures before you read the story and discuss what is happening, how the characters might feel, and what the characters can do about their feelings. If you are reading a chapter book, you can begin each session by recalling what happened at the end of the previous chapter, and how the character felt about the situation.

Model talking about feelings. You can model noticing specific information about feelings (for example, feelings change or feelings are different from action), or you can model how you handle feelings or the problem you face. Verbalizing your feelings, how you calm yourself, and how you solve problems are powerful tools. Explain what happened, how you felt, and what you did or will do about the situation, as Carol does below.

My son Robby had a terrible temper, which, I'm sad to say, he may have gotten from me. I decided it was unreasonable to expect Robby to deal with his anger if I let it all hang out. Since I often got mad driving, I decided to practice calming myself in the car. The next time someone cut me off I said, "Did you see that? He cut me off. I am so angry I could explode. I'm going to take deep breaths and calm down." Breathe, breathe, breathe. Then I stopped taking deep breaths to see if I was calm. I looked into myself and said, "Oh, I'm still angry. I need to take some more breaths." I continued taking breaths until I felt calm.

Once I was calm, I said, "I was really angry, and I'm calm now," and then told Robby that it didn't help anything when I yelled at the other drivers, so

I was beginning to learn how to calm myself by taking deep breaths. I also invited him to remind me to breathe if he thought I was getting mad, which he shyly did.

Interestingly, a couple of weeks later his sister knocked his blocks down. He started to yell at her, stopped, and took three deep breaths. Then he turned to me and said, "I'm calmer, too."

Carol not only calmed herself down, but she explained why she was doing it and invited her son to help her. He got to think about using breathing to calm down without the stress of having to do it. That gave him the confidence to try it himself.

It is also helpful to model how you solve problems that upset you, as Becky's experience demonstrates below.

I was having a very difficult time balancing the checkbook. The sound of my kids (ages 6 and 9) quarreling over the rules of a board game increased my stress. I debated whether to intervene or let them work it out.

Finally I got up and went into where they were squabbling and said, "Let's see, I am trying to balance the checkbook and the kids' quarreling is distracting me. What can I do? I could take away the game, I could send them outside, I could cover them with a blanket to deaden the sound, or make a soundproof booth to put them in, I could . . ." My son interrupted my problem-solving process and said, "Go away, Mom, we'll take care of it." And they did.

Becky modeled using the problem-solving process to solve her frustration. She also let her children solve their own problem. This approach simply involves saying out loud what you are thinking – and perhaps editing your language a bit.

When children feel good about themselves and are comfortable thinking about feelings, they can more easily respond to the hurtful teasing of other children. This can be seen in the following example.

Zhao Hui was a lively 7-year-old. She was born in China, adopted as a baby, and raised in the United States. Some of the kids at school were teasing her, saying, "Chinese people are stupid and they eat worms." When Zhao Hui's mother heard about the teasing, she asked Zhao Hui how she felt about it. Zhao Hui said, "I'm Chinese and I don't eat worms. They're just silly." In this situation, Zhao Hui was able to reframe the message from hurtful to silly.

In addition to general information about feelings, children sometimes need help with specific situations that happen over and over again.

ᗡ Working with challenging problems

When your child has a problem that requires action – whether it is new or recurring, you need a plan. An effective plan identifies the problem and skills the child needs, teaches those skills when the child is calm, and practices using them in pretend. When the child can use the skills in pretend situations, you can encourage using them in real situations. Finally, review your plan – notice what went well and what can be improved. We can see how the process works step-by-step with the example below.

Identify the problem and skills needed. When a child gets very angry, try to determine what the cause is. It may be something that happened or it may be an interpretation the child made. When you have an idea, decide what the child needs in order to respond differently – basic information about the nature of feelings, or skills to handle the feelings or situation. Often, you will have to play detective.

Seven-year-old Ellie and Hanna were playing at Ellie's house. Suddenly Hanna announced that Ellie was not her friend anymore. Nothing had happened to precipitate this announcement. Ellie was crushed and began to cry. The more Hanna said Ellie wasn't her friend, the more Ellie sobbed. After unsuccessfully trying to reconcile the girls, Lynn, Ellie's mom, asked Hanna's mother to come and get her.

After thinking about the situation, Lynn remembered that this had happened last time Hanna was there, and also when Ellie visited Hanna. Lynn concluded that Hanna told Ellie that she wasn't her friend anymore to get a rise out of Ellie, not because she actually disliked her. Lynn decided Ellie needed to learn how to calm herself and respond to the situation.

Teach the needed skills. If possible, avoid the problem while you are teaching the skill or information the child needs and the child is practicing. When the child has developed some skill in pretend, you can prompt the child to use the skill in a real situation before she is very upset.

Lynn concluded that Ellie was a sensitive child who needed to develop a little backbone or she would be walked all over. She decided to work with Ellie before Hanna came over again on how to be able to calm herself so she didn't cry, and how to respond to Hanna's comments in such a way that she retained her dignity.

Lynn wanted her daughter to know that Hanna was trying to get her upset and that the more she cried, the more Hanna would bait her. She told her the story about two fish.

> Two fish were swimming in the water hunting for food. They came to a wiggling worm. The red fish said, "That's not a good worm." But the orange fish swam closer anyway and said, "It looks good to me." The red fish warned him, "Don't eat it – a hook's attached." The orange fish ate it anyway, and the fisherman jerked him out of the water.

Lynn said to her daughter, "Hanna is trying to jerk you around just like the fisherman jerked the fish around. When you respond to her mean words, she is controlling you just like the fisherman controls the orange fish. You can decide if you want to be jerked around or not. Is that what you want?" Ellie shook her head "No." Lynn said, "Then let's practice saying 'No' to 'worm' words."

Although Ellie knew how to take deep breaths when she was frustrated, it did not seem to be enough when her friends were mean. Lynn decided to teach her to say to herself, "I am a good person even if ____ is being mean." Lynn decided she would first introduce the concept by telling Ellie a story from work, then act it out, saying, "I'm a good person . . ." with puppets. At first, Lynn would play both parts and then Ellie would help the puppets use self-talk and decide what to do. The puppets would learn to respond to several types of 'mean talk.' Finally, Lynn and Ellie would act out the situation with Hanna in pretend. When Ellie was able to stay calm during practice, Lynn decided that they were ready for a child to visit.

Retry the situation. Let your child use new skills in the problem situation. It is helpful if she can be rested and relaxed when you reintroduce the situation. When she tries, praise her for either effort or success.

First, Lynn invited over Ellie's cousin Sonya. Sonya tended to be thoughtless but was not deliberately mean. Lynn planned to stay nearby so she could prompt Ellie if she needed it. When Sonya told Ellie that her hair was ugly, Ellie's face began to cloud up. Lynn stepped in view and make a fish-swimming motion with her hands. Ellie began to smile and told her cousin, "Well, it's a good thing it's not on your head". Her cousin laughed and things proceeded pleasantly.

That visit went so well that Lynn was willing to invite Hanna over. Again the girls played happily for about 45 minutes, and then Hanna told Ellie that she wasn't her friend anymore. Ellie's face started to cloud again, Lynn made the swimming motion with her hand, Ellie took a slow breath, and said, "Okay. If you don't want to be friends, my mother can take you home now." Hanna looked baffled and said, "Don't you want me to play with you?" Ellie replied, "Not if you're going to say mean things," and handed Hanna her coat.

Lynn and Ellie took Hanna home. When they returned, Lynn asked, "How do you feel?"

"A little sad, and a little happy."

Lynn asked, "What are you sad about?"

"I really did want to play, but not if she is mean."

"And what are you happy about?"

"I didn't let her jerk me like the orange fish," Ellie said with a grin.

"Is there something you would do differently next time?" Lynn asked.

"I don't know. Why?"

Exercise 7-1:
Make a plan

Instructions: Pick a problem and work through the steps below.

Identify the problem and needed skills.
Briefly describe the last time the situation happened.

Why do you think your child has difficulty with this situation?

What skills or information does your child need to respond differently?

Teach needed skills. How will you –
Teach the skill?

Link the skill to feelings?

Practice the skill in pretend?

Retry in a real situation
When you choose to introduce the skill, what will you need to be aware of?

How will you introduce the skill in a real situation?

Review the plan and results
What worked?
What can be improved?

"Because when you have a problem with someone it is good to think about what you want to do next time if it happens again," said Lynn.

Review the situation. Was it handled successfully? What strategy needs more work? What aspect of the situation needs a new approach?

Lynn reflected, "Overall, things went very well. Practice with the puppets took a long time. Inviting Sonya over was a good idea. It gave Ellie a chance to practice before Hanna came again. I think that we need to act out more situations with puppets."

In this example, Lynn took the time to identify the problem and make a plan to help Ellie deal with mean comments. She also took the time to teach the skills Ellie needed and to practice, practice, practice with her.

ℒ Another challenging situation

Sometimes a child's learning is made more difficult by family circumstances. When situations are very difficult, the child's emotional reserve is wiped out and he or she cannot handle even routine events, as Calvin demonstrates below.

Calvin (age 5) was living with his grandmother because his mother was seriously, perhaps terminally, ill and his father was too distraught to care for him. Calvin was very confused and angry. He missed his mom, and his dad would say he was coming and not show up. Or, Dad would come, say things were going to be okay and Calvin could come home soon, and then nothing would change.

His grandmother took the brunt of his anger. One Monday Calvin came home from kindergarten and demanded a banana. When she said they didn't have any bananas, he started to hit her. He had been fine when he left for school, so his response was unexpected.

Identify the problem and needed skills. *Grandma enfolded him in a big hug so he could not hurt her and asked what had happened at school that morning. He burst into tears and explained that the sun was shining and he had planned to play on the playground with Joey and Martin. But the teacher had special plans and they didn't go out at all. He had managed to hold himself together until he got home, but not having a banana he wanted was just too much to bear.*

Grandma could feel the anger and disappointment boiling within Calvin, so she said that the sun was still shining and asked him if he wanted to go out back and play with Sandy, their dog. He said yes, and went and played for an hour before returning for lunch.

While he was outside, Grandma thought about the situation. Calvin's dad had visited the day before but he had been very distracted. Clearly, what little emotional reserves Calvin had were gone and his emotional bucket was overflowing with anger. She decided to do two things – one, see that he got much more physical activity, and two, teach him some self-calming tools to use at school.

Teach needed skills. *Grandma decided to teach Calvin to take deep breaths and blow out all the tension. To do this she started blowing "tissues balls" down the table. The bigger the breath, the faster the tissue would roll. Calvin played, too, and enjoyed seeing whose ball would win.*

One day after they had been blowing a long time, she said, "I feel really calm after all that blowing. It's like I blew out all my frustrations. How about you?" When he agreed, she suggested they pretend they were mad at the dog because she chewed Calvin's baseball and they could blow the mads out.

They continued to play "Let's pretend" for several days. Then she told him, "If you think I need to calm down, wave a tissue at me, and I'll remember to take breaths." He would sometimes wave a tissue at her for fun and she would take breaths.

Retry in a real situation. *One Saturday they were visiting a friend's house and the friend would not share his bike. Calvin got mad and Grandma got out a tissue and waved it. Calvin looked surprised and then took in a big breath and slowly let it out.*

The next day Calvin's dad came over but just sat on the chair and would not play Chinese checkers with Calvin. Soon he left and Calvin began knocking things off the shelves. Grandma waved a tissue but he continued to knock things off the shelves. She picked him up squirming and took him out back where they played tag until they were both exhausted.

Review the plan and results. *When they finally came in, Grandma reflected on Calvin's progress. Taking breaths helped with friends, however, it did not help with Dad. She decided she would continue to encourage breathing, and she would need to find a way to get more exercise into Calvin's routine. She would also have to see what she could do to help Calvin's dad be more responsive.*

Children need information about feelings, and tools to calm themselves and to deal with the situations they face. Parents can introduce this information by modeling talking about their feelings. They can also make plans to teach children specific skills they need to deal with the situations they face. Parents can provide this help more easily if they can remain calm when their children are upset. We will discuss that in the next chapter.

Chapter Eight

Staying calm when kids are upset

Another effective way to help children deal with their disappointment is to remain calm when they are upset. To stay calm, you need to understand why you might get upset, how you might get drawn into the child's distress, and how you could take care of yourself so that you can remain separate.

✍❧ *Identify your emotional triggers*

When children get angry, parents sometimes get angry, too. Once the crisis has passed, it helps to reflect on why you were upset. When you identify emotional triggers, whether from the past or present, you can begin to deal with them.

Present issues. Parents, like children, get angry more easily when they are hungry, tired, ignored, or stressed. Annoying habits like whistling off key or cracking knuckles become much harder to tolerate when you are tired. The dawdling that you can usually accept becomes intolerable when you are tired or have a deadline to meet, as seen below.

I don't know why it is that whenever I'm late my children are extremely slow. If I try to speed them up, they move slower still. If I offer to help or give them choices, they cry or scream. Then I become really angry because I am trying to be reasonable and they aren't cooperating.

Identify common themes and find ways to avoid the problem or take emotional care of yourself so you do not get upset. You can find ideas later in this chapter in the section "Take Care of Yourself."

Stress can come from financial worries, work troubles, or difficulties with a relationship. Each of these situations drains a person's emotional resources. When you add a distressed child, your remaining emotional resources are exhausted.

The cure for emotional exhaustion is to get the help you need – talk to a friend, marriage counselor, therapist, financial manager, or debt counselor. When your problems are being dealt with, you will probably be able to accept your children's distress more calmly.

Past issues. A person's experience as a child may cast a shadow on his or her experience as a parent. If you grew up in a household where your parents yelled at you, you might feel angry and helpless when your child yells at you. If your older sister was mean to you, you might get very angry when your older child is mean to your younger child. The past can influence the present in surprising ways, as Rebecca discovered.

Rebecca was talking to some friends. She told them how mad she got when her three-year-old son snitched the pepperoni from her pizza. She asked her friends for ideas on how to make him stop. Her description was so intense that one friend asked, "Has anything like this ever happened to you before?" Rebecca thought a moment and said, "Yes. When I was a child, my brother would take food from my plate and my parents never made him stop." Then she smiled and added, "Oh, I'm the parent now. I can handle this."

The anger and helplessness Rebecca felt as a parent was rooted in her childhood experience. When she identified the problem and realized she was now the adult, she could handle the situation. Not all problems are solved as easily as this, but understanding the origin can be helpful. In some cases you may be able to simply let go of the problem, as Rebecca did, when you know what it is. In other cases, you may need to actively forgive your parents or someone else or seek counseling.

✐ *Remain emotionally separate*

It is easy for parents to get caught up in their children's joys and frustrations. If a child's classmate says, "I won't be your friend," it may bring back a parent's pain of childhood rejection. If a child is panicking because he can't find his homework paper, it may be hard for some parents to stay calm and separate. A parent may feel livid and personally insulted when his child is cut from the soccer team if Dad is personally invested in a sports career for his son.

Is this my problem? If you find yourself wanting to get involved with your child's turmoil, ask yourself, "Is this my problem?" "Who created the problem?" "Whose needs are not being met?" If your son created the problem by not putting his homework away and if he – not you – needs the paper, then it is his problem. If you become upset when he panics, look for ways to maintain your composure and help him deal with his problem.

When parents become emotionally over-involved in their children's lives, they often see and feel things as a child again, rather than maintaining an adult perspective. This hinders their ability to offer their children the necessary support. Further, children often take their cues from

Exercise 8-1:
Who's sorry now?

Instructions: Read each sentence and decide whether or not the parent is responsible for the situation he or she is sorry for. If the parent is *responsible,* circle "Okay." If the parent is *not responsible,* circle "Revise" and rewrite the statement to acknowledge the child's feelings.

Okay / Revise   1. I'm sorry Josh didn't invite you to his birthday party.

Okay / Revise   2. I'm sorry I knocked over your block tower.

Okay / Revise   3. You really worked hard on the paper. I'm sorry your teacher gave you a poor grade.

Okay / Revise   4. I'm sorry I yelled at you for spilling your milk.

Okay / Revise   5. I wish Grandma had given you what you wanted for your birthday.

Possible answers: 1. *Revise.* I can see you are hurt that Josh didn't invite you to his birthday party. 2. *Ok.* The parent was at fault. 3. *Revise.* You're disappointed that you got a poor grade on the paper you worked so hard on. 4. *Ok.* The parent was at fault. 5. *Revise.* You are sad Grandma didn't send you what you wanted.

grown-ups as to how bad the situation really is. When their parents are greatly distressed, children's distress will increase also.

Think before saying "I'm sorry." Remaining emotionally separate means acknowledging your child's feeling without introducing your own. One way parents insert their feelings is to say, "I'm sorry that . . . " By inserting the "I'm sorry," you switch the focus from the child's feelings to your feelings. For example, "I'm so sorry your friend was mean." When that happens, the child often begins to worry about her parent as well as the original problem.

There are times when it is appropriate to say "I'm sorry." When you have done something hurtful or wrong, it is appropriate to apologize. For example, if you blamed Tommy for the mess his brother made or yelled at Sarah for no reason, it is appropriate to apologize. In exercise 8-1 you have a chance to identify whether "I'm sorry" is appropriate.

How do you know if you are too involved? It is reasonable to be invested in your child's well-being. In fact, studies have shown that children do better in school when parents are involved. However, when parents' actions discourage children from learning or when parents protect their children from the consequences of the children's actions, the parents are too involved. Here are three questions you can ask yourself to evaluate your level of involvement.

1. *Do you move in to help your child before she has tried to resolve the issue herself?* This can be by comforting her, defending her, smoothing her path, or doing something she could have done herself.

2. *Do you grant your child's wishes or requests even when they are difficult or inconvenient for you?* This can be giving children what they want or doing what they want. Children need to learn to negotiate and, also, to set their needs aside for others. When they consistently get what they want, they begin to feel that everyone should please them all the time.

3. *Is your child your primary source of pleasure?* It is appropriate to be delighted in your child's growth and accomplishments. However, if he or she is your only source of pleasure you are probably over-involved.

To explore this issue more, read *The Too Precious Child: The Perils of Being a Super-Parent and How to Avoid Them* by Lynne H. Williams.

ℒ♥ *Remain in charge of your feelings*

When some people are angry, they unknowingly blame their anger on their children, as in "You made me mad when you bounced the ball inside." Or, "When you poke your sister, you make me furious." In both of these examples the parent has given the child control of her feelings with the phrase "You made me." It is difficult enough for most children to control their own feelings; it is unreasonable for a parent to put her children in charge of her feelings as well.

Instead the parent could say, "When you bounce the ball inside, I feel angry." Or, "I get furious when you poke your sister. You know it is not okay to hurt people." In the following exercise, see if you can identify the statements where the parent gives away control of her feelings.

Exercise 8-2:
Who's in charge of the feelings?

Instructions: Read each sentence and decide who is in charge. If the *parent* is in charge of his or her feelings, circle the P. If the *child* is in charge of the parent's feelings, circle the C and rewrite the statement to put the parent in charge.

P / C   1. If you don't go to bed now, you will make me very sad.

P / C   2. I feel angry when I ask you to hang up your coat and you don't do it.

P / C   3. I told you not to turn on the TV. You turned it on anyway. You made me very mad.

P / C   4. You set the table without asking. I am happy you remembered.

P / C   5. You've made me so happy. Thank you for the valentine.

P / C   6. I feel frustrated when you leave all your toys on the floor.

P / C   7. When you do something that I have told you not to do, you make me feel angry.

Possible answers: 1. child in charge: Go to bed now. 2. parent in charge. 3. child in charge: I am mad that you turned the TV on when I asked you not to. 4. parent in charge. 5. child in charge: I felt happy when I read the valentine from you. 6. parent in charge. 7. child in charge: I feel angry when you do something I have told you not to do.

✐ *Maintain your self-esteem*

People with high self-esteem feel lovable and capable. Anger often arises when one's self-esteem is threatened – that is, when you don't feel lovable or capable. Jean Illsley Clarke has an interesting discussion about this in her book *Growing Up Again: Parenting Ourselves, Parenting Our Children*. Parenting often challenges one's self-esteem, particularly if your child is prone to angry outbursts, wrenching sobs, or saying, "I hate you."

When you get angry or caught up in your child's distress, it helps to step back and decide if your "lovableness" or your "capableness" are being threatened. Below, Aaron's mom's capableness is threatened.

Eighteen-month-old Aaron wanted to draw on the wall with marking pens. Mom tried to interest him in using the paper she put out on the floor, but he continued to scream. She then tried to interest him in another activity, but he still screamed. She held him in her arms for a bit and he continued to scream. Finally she put him on the floor. He ran back, picked up the marker, and scribbled on the wall before she could stop him.

It is easy to see how Mom might feel incompetent and angry when Aaron wrote on the wall the second time. She offered him an appropriate place to draw, tried to redirect him, and even held him as he cried – and nothing worked.

Parents sometimes feel angry when they feel unloved, as Henrietta found.

Henrietta had grown up in a harsh, unloving family. She had gone through therapy before deciding to have children. She wanted a better life for her son, David, so she was very selective about the people who cared for him.

One day when Henrietta came home from work, her two-and-a-half year-old son looked up from playing with his babysitter and said, "Go away. I hate you." When Henrietta stood dumbfounded, David tried to push his mother out of the house. Henrietta was furious. She was trying to make a good life for David and he didn't want her around.

Henrietta felt furious because David didn't appear to love her. On reflection, Henrietta realized that what David probably meant was, "I'm having fun right now and I don't want the babysitter to go home." Further, Henrietta could congratulate herself both on finding a caring babysitter and on David's willingness to express his feelings – something that she would never have dared to do in the family she grew up in. Once she realized that David really did love her, her anger subsided.

When you feel angry, check to see if you are feeling unloved or inca-pable. Then check whether the feeling of being unloved or incapable is appropriate. Take comfort in the knowledge that when you raise children, many of the things you try will fail or backfire and that does not make you either unlovable or incapable.

When you do find yourself getting angry, it helps to either deal with the root cause, past or present, or take care of yourself so you can withstand the emotional stress.

ℒ⊸ Take care of yourself

Taking care of yourself can be broken into two parts – acting on the things you can influence, and letting go of the things you have no control over. The following are a number of things you can do.

Talk to someone. That someone can be a friend, pastor, counselor, or relative – someone who can acknowledge your feelings and help you see your choices more clearly.

Check your facts. Sometimes anger is based on incorrect information or assumptions, as with Henrietta above. Determine why you're feeling angry, and decide if it is reasonable to feel that way.

Revise your expectation. Anger and stress often come from unrealistic expectations. When people try to keep an orderly home, serve elaborate meals, be a wonderful parent, have a satisfying relationship, maintain an exciting career, and be a supportive friend, they are usually unrealistic. Sometimes you will need to let some things slip. You might lower your housekeeping standards, serve simple meals, or turn down a project at work. A classic example is the mother, below, who wanted to make Christmas perfect.

I wanted to make a perfect Christmas for my children when they were young. I was making homemade gifts for everyone, baking cookies, writing Christmas cards, and planning the grand Christmas dinner. The harder I worked, the more my children quarreled and cried. I got so angry because I was trying to make it perfect for them and they were getting in the way.

It wasn't until after Christmas that I realized my kids didn't care about perfect, they only wanted to spend time with me. I made plans then to scale back the next year and to involve my children in what I did. It was still tough the following year but much better.

Get help. That may involve reading a book, taking an anger management or parenting class, finding a mentor, getting counseling, or even talking to a lawyer. Get new information so you can respond differently.

Plan time for yourself. Most people need a little time for themselves each day to spend doing something they enjoy or doing absolutely nothing at all. With children this is called "hanging loose." Personal time is not for doing something you "should" do, like study for a French exam, repair the car, or plan the meals for next week. The time can be as little as 15 or 20 minutes. Some parents get personal time by rising earlier in the morning, or stopping for a latte on the way home from work. Find what works for you.

Use positive self-talk. Monitor what you say about yourself both out loud and mentally. For example, some parents use negative talk like, "I'm a lousy parent. Alex still has tantrums all the time, " or "I can never do anything right – the house is a total mess." Self-talk can influence your mind and create what you say, with positive or negative results.

Change negative self-talk by replacing the negative phrase with a positive one. Four ways to do this are to remind yourself that (1) You are lovable even though you're not perfect, (2) You are capable even though things are not going well right now, (3) You are growing and getting better, and (4) You do "it" well sometimes, as shown by a specific success. These four approaches to changes can be seen in the chart below.

"I'm a lousy parent. Alex still has tantrums all the time."	
Lovable affirmation	"I am lovable even when Alex yells at me."
Growing affirmation	"I am learning different ways to help Alex so he can do things himself."
Capable affirmation	"Alex has fewer tantrums than he used to have."
Positive example	"Alex went one hour without getting upset once."

"I can never do anything right – the house is a total mess."	
Loveable affirmation	"My husband and children love me even though the house is a mess."
Growing affirmation	"I am developing strategies to reduce clutter in the house."
Capable affirmation	"I choose to spend time with my kids. I get the house tidy when company is coming."
Positive example	"The house stayed tidy for two whole days last time I cleaned it up."

Changing negative self-talk to positive self-talk promotes positive change. The change, although real, is gradual. You can practice changing negative self-talk with exercise 8-3.

Exercise 8-3:
Changing self-talk

Instructions: Read each sentence and revise the negative self-talk to positive self-talk in two different ways.

1. My house is always a mess. I'm a rotten housekeeper.
   - _____
   - _____

2. Alex always cries when I try to help him. I can never do anything right.
   - _____
   - _____

3. I can't get anywhere on time. I'm always late.
   - _____
   - _____

4. If I were a good parent, Megan wouldn't get so angry all the time.
   - _____
   - _____

5. I must be a bad parent. My child still wets the bed / has tantrums or

   _____.
   - _____
   - _____

Possible answers: 1. *Messy house.* "I choose to spend time with my children." *Or,* "I can clean the house when company is coming." 2. *Child leaves crying.* "I am a capable person even when my child gets upset with me." *Or,* "I am trying different ways of working with my child. 3. *Always late.* "I can arrive on time when it is important to me." *Or,* "I was on time to the doctor's office yesterday." 4. *I'm a bad parent.* "I'm a good parent, even though Megan gets mad at me." *Or,* "I am learning new ways to talk to Megan." 5. *Child wets the bed.* "I have taken my child to the doctor to see if something is wrong physically." *Or,* "I am a lovable, capable parent even though my daughter wets her bed."

Table 8-1:
"Instant" calming strategies

Physical	Take a long deep breath and slowly blow it out. Stand still, arms by your sides, and take five deep breaths. Sit down on the floor or ground (lower than your child) and take deep breaths. Turn away from your child and walk 20 steps or go into another room. Go to the sink and get a drink of water. Shake your hands as if to let the anger drip off.
Auditory/ verbal	Self-talk: Say, "I am the adult. I can handle this respectfully." Or, say, "This, too, will pass." Count backwards from 10 to 1. Say the alphabet backwards. Detach from the crisis and notice the background sounds – wind blowing or the hum of an appliance. Think about how you can make the situation into a humorous story.
Visual/ mental	Turn and look out a window or away from the chaos. Notice the color and texture of the clouds or walls. Visualize your child's anger dripping off you like water off a duck's back. Or, visualize your anger settling out like the sediment in a jar of muddy water. Imagine yourself as a trained safety professional – go mental in the face of high emotion, maintaining a calm attitude and quiet voice. Turn your thoughts inward and gently observe and accept your feelings without attempting to change them. Repeat a mantra over and over, and visualize it until you feel calm.

ℐ♥ *Use calming techniques yourself*

Self-calming tools can be used when you feel yourself getting angry or they can be used as a preventive. Think about the things you do. What do you do that makes you feel particularly calm or good?

When you look for ideas, collect both "instant" calming tools and "general" calming ideas. Instant calming tools are strategies you can use immediately. They don't need any special props or space. You can find examples in the table above.

Table 8-2:
"General" or preventive calming strategies

Physical	Walk, jog, work out. Clean a closet, organize a room, weed the garden, wash the car, mow the lawn, make repairs, go for a bike ride, do yoga.
Auditory/ verbal	Talk to a friend. Listen to music – either soothing or rousing, depending on your needs. Listen to a book on tape.
Visual	Read a book, watch the sunset, visualize your stress drifting away, meditate. Visit an art gallery. Surf the Internet.
Creative	Bake bread, write in a journal, sew or knit, take photos, draw or paint, build something. Work a crossword puzzle, do a physical puzzle (Rubik's cube). Play an instrument – with music or improvising.
Self- nurturing	Get a latte or cup of hot cocoa or tea, take a long warm shower or bath, sit back and sip a glass of wine. Eat a favorite dessert. Buy a new tool or gadget. Visit a book store.
Humor	Watch a silly movie, read a funny story. Go through a collection of cartoons. Listen to a comedy recording or tape. Visit an Internet humor site.

General calming tools can be used for prevention or for restoring calm. You can use prevention strategies to reduce your overall tension between storms. That way you will have more emotional stamina to deal with your child's next outburst. As a restorative, you can use them after the storm has passed to help you completely calm down and release the residual frustration and anger. Above is a list of general calming strategies parents have suggested.

✐ *Reduce clutter*

For many people, clutter and confusion create a background of stress. As long as everything is smooth there is no problem. When time or tempers get short, the clutter adds stress. Reducing clutter has two elements: creating order and maintaining order.

Create order. The old saying, "A place for everything, and every-thing in its place" has merit. It reduces your daughter's hunt for her book report and your search for car keys. When your child knows where to find her soccer socks and blue sweater, your job of remaining separate is easier. There are a number of good books on getting organized. You can find a few listed in Appendix E. However, getting organized is just the beginning; you also need to learn to keep order.

Maintain order. Once you have your things in order, the challenge is to keep things orderly. Two tips: limit the volume of stuff you collect, and develop the habit of putting things away. You can limit intake by des-ignating a specific volume, for example, one box of toy cars, three shelves of books, or one doll per year of age. Or, you can use the "one-in-one-out" approach. That is, every time you get a toy or shirt, you need to give away one. When you decrease the clutter, you decrease the need to rescue your kids. Again, more ideas can be found in books on getting organized.

ℐ↩ *Develop an action plan*

Emotional meltdowns of children sometimes come as a surprise. However, there is often a pattern when you look for it. Similarly, parents are sometimes surprised at how angry they can become at their children. Look at those times and notice what they have in common.

If you have trouble remembering, keep notes on a calendar or in a notebook. For example, many parents get angry when they are trying to get kids to bed or out the door in the morning and their children slow them down. It can be a two-year-old's insistence that her socks are on "just so," or a 12-year-old's search for his gym clothes. One way to remain calm and separate is to have an action plan. Such a plan needs two ele-ments – ways to deal with the situation and ways to calm yourself.

Dealing with the situations. When you are dealing with a frus-trating situation, it helps to brainstorm ideas. That means to write down all the ideas you can think of, then think of adding new silly or creative ideas. Generally, the best ideas come after you run out of ideas the first time, because the ideas you record at first are usually ones you have con-sidered. If they were going to work, they already would have.

Several books have lists of brainstorming already done for parents – *365 Wacky, Wonderful Ways to Get Your Child to Do What You Want* by Elizabeth Crary and the *Help!* Series by Jean Illsley Clarke and others. *Love & Limits* by Elizabeth Crary also introduces a simple approach for brainstorming. This approach has three specific tools for each of five points. When you apply all the tools to the problem, you have 15 ideas. Ideas from this five-point approach are presented in the table below.

Table 8-3:
Brainstorming for ideas to handle a situation

Problem: My 3½-year-old son whines whenever he wants me to do (or get) something for him. I need ideas on how to deal with him.

Note: The ideas below were generated by using the tools from STAR Parenting. For more about STAR Parenting, read *Love & Limits* by Elizabeth Crary (see Appendix E).

Avoid the problem
- Go for a run each day to reduce stress for both of you.
- Buy ear plugs and use them to reduce the volume of whining.

Set age-appropriate limits
- Say, "When you whine the answer will be 'No.'" *Note:* You must be willing to follow through with the consequences or this will not work.
- Give a consequence. "If you whine, you must leave the room. You may return when you can use a pleasant voice."

Teach new skills
- Model speaking pleasantly – even when you feel upset.
- Break the task of "speaking pleasantly" into small steps. (1) Identify unpleasant (whining) voices in other people. (2) Notice when he is using a whiny voice. (3) Ask him to change his voice when he starts to whine. And finally, (4) ask him to start speaking pleasantly.
- Model re-doing it right – When you yell or whine, model changing your voice. Say, "Oops, that was my whiny voice. This is my pleasant voice."

Acknowledge feelings
- "You must be frustrated trying to tell me something."
- "Wouldn't it be fun if the whole kitchen were filled with cookies and you had to eat your way out."

Respond to cooperation
- Give him your full attention when he is pleasant.
- Say, "Thank you so much for using a pleasant voice. Now I know what you want."
- The first couple of times he asks without whining, give him what he wants immediately.

Dealing with the feelings. The second part of developing an action plan is to decide how you will calm yourself when you get angry or upset. There are two reasons to have a plan: first, there are some situations that you can't change, you can only change your response. And second, children take on the emotional energy of their parents. If you are angry, it will be harder for your child to decide what to do about his or her situation and feelings.

To get ideas to calm yourself in a crisis you can review the instant calming strategies or the general self-calming tools discussed earlier in this chapter. You can also talk to a wise friend, make plans to see a counselor, or take an anger management course.

Once you have some ideas on how to calm yourself when your child has a major tantrum, write them down on a piece of paper. Then, you are ready to make your action plan.

The plan. The third step is to create the action plan itself. To do that, look at your list of brainstorming ideas for the situation and select one or two ideas you could try next time your child is upset. Then look at your list of self-calming ideas and decide on one or two instant calming ideas you can use to soothe yourself if you become angry in the middle of the storm.

Once you know what you want to do when your child is upset, think about what general self-soothing things you can do beforehand to make the "crisis" time easier. For example, if you want to use music to calm your child or yourself, decide what music you will use and put it near the player so you won't have to hunt for it. If you decide that getting more physical exercise would help your child deal with disappointments, your plan would include how and when you are going to provide the exercise.

When you have worked out these ideas, write them down on your action plan. Post the plan where you will most likely need it. If necessary, make a couple of copies to put in different places. The following is an action plan developed by Lynn.

Lynn was a foster parent for six-year-old Theodore. He was a delightful child who had significant separation issues that made bedtimes difficult at best. He did not want to be left alone and would resort to furious outbursts and clever manipulations to resist going to bed. He would knock all the toys off the shelves, throw things, hit or kick Lynn, or cry desperately that he was scared or needed something. It was hard to sort out genuine need from manipulative behavior. It took a great deal of personal strength not to retaliate.

By trial and error, Lynn learned that leniency toward behavior and flexibility in routine were not working. Theodore needed a very simple, kind and firm, predictable bedtime routine. The problem for Lynn was she knew the transition to a new bedtime routine would be physically and emotionally exhausting.

She developed a simple evening routine that could be followed fairly rigidly and that allowed time for connecting emotionally. She had noticed that Theodore was calmer when he had a great deal of physical activity. So she decided to make the transition on a three-day weekend when they would have time for hiking, biking, and swimming. She also noted that rocking calmed Theodore, as it did her.

Lynn was usually able to keep her frustration in check by thinking about her long-term goal for Theodore – having him go to bed peacefully at an appropriate hour. However, she knew that if he put up his usual fuss at a change in routine, she would need more than long-term goals to keep herself calm.

Lynn's action plan

When I change Theodore's bedtime routine I will:
• Tell him what the new rules for bedtime are.
• Deal with his anger by holding him firmly to prevent him hurting me and by rocking him to calm him.
• Deal with my intense feelings by standing still and taking deep breaths first, and then drowning out his noise by chanting over and over to myself, "Peace flows like a river."

Before I put him to bed the first night I will:
• Move the rocker into his room.
• Make sure he has had a snack *before* I say it's time for bed.
• Remind myself that I know what to do if I become angry.
• Plan something enjoyable to do with the extra quiet time I have after getting him to bed successfully.

Right now I'll tape my action plan high on his door, so it's handy when I need it. I will also write down what works or doesn't so I can adjust my strategy as needed.

You can use the forms in Exercises 8-4 and 8-5 as guides in creating your own action plan. If you use the plan and it does not work, you can create as many new plans as you need to find something that works.

In this chapter, we have looked at how to stay calm when kids are upset. This involves understanding why you are angry, looking at ways to calm yourself, and developing an action plan to deal with common problems. In the next chapter, we will look at how long you try to teach your child to deal with disappointment, and what to do when your effort does not work.

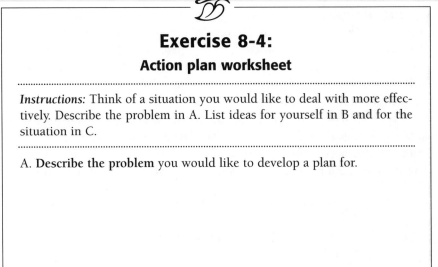

Exercise 8-4:
Action plan worksheet

Instructions: Think of a situation you would like to deal with more effectively. Describe the problem in A. List ideas for yourself in B and for the situation in C.

A. **Describe the problem** you would like to develop a plan for.

B. List ideas for yourself.
Why do you think you get angry when your child is upset? What are past or present influences? Do you feel lovable and capable?

C. List ideas for the situation.
What do you want your child to do instead of what he or she does?

Exercise 8-5:
Action plan

Instructions: Create an action plan for the problem you described in Exercise 8-4. Begin by reviewing your answers, then record below what you will do both *before* your child is upset and *when* he or she is upset.

Next time my child is upset I will:

• Deal with the *situation* by –

• Deal with my *feelings* by (instant calm) –

Before my child is upset I will do the following things for:

• My child –

• Myself –

Right now I will put the plan _____ so it's handy when I need it.

Chapter Nine

Questions and answers

We have looked at why understanding the nature of feelings is important, how to teach children skills to deal with both their feelings and the situation, and what people can do to remain calm when their children are upset. In this chapter we will look at how long it takes to teach children to deal with disappointment, what to do when your effort does not work, and some questions parents have about helping kids deal with disappointment.

How long does it take?

How long does it take to teach kids to deal with their feelings? The answer is – it depends. The usual range is six months to a year or so. It depends on the child's temperament, age, experiences, and parental modeling. We will look at each of these elements briefly.

Temperament. Research into temperament traits has identified several traits that affect the expression of feelings: mood, intensity of response, and emotional sensitivity.

Mood. Mood is the way a person views the world. Some children are born happy most of the time; others, grumpy much of the time. Most children, of course, have happy and grumpy times. Children who are grumpy more often will need to understand that they have a choice in how they view the world and will probably need more tools to cope with their feelings than a child whose temperament is happy.

Intensity. Some children are born intense, others mellow. In the newborn nursery of some hospitals some babies' cries can barely be heard, others' reverberate to the end of the hall. If your child has always been intense, she will need more time to learn self-coping skills than if she has always been mellow.

Emotional sensitivity. Some children are super aware of their own feelings, some are more aware of others' feelings, and some are oblivious to feelings altogether. Children who are not tuned into their feelings may get angry, but not have any idea why. The more you need to teach your child about feelings and coping skills, the longer the process usually takes. Several books that can help you figure out your child's temperament are included in Appendix E.

Age. Many parents have the impression that children cannot learn about feelings until somewhere between three and six years, however, children can learn much earlier than that. The optimal time to learn about feelings is 12 to 36 months.

Self-soothing. Dr. William Sears, a noted pediatrician, says that between six to nine months babies can begin to learn to soothe themselves – with a little help from parents. And, further, mellow babies tend to soothe themselves earlier than intense babies.

Developmental tasks. In *Self-Esteem: A Family Affair,* Jean Illsley Clarke writes that the job of a child 18 to 36 months old is to learn to think for herself and to learn about using feelings. From this perspective, two-year-old tantrums can be seen as the child's struggle to learn about feelings. If parents help, either consciously or unconsciously, the child passes through the stage. If the child cannot figure out how to use his feelings appropriately, his angry behavior will continue into the next developmental stage.

Experiences. Several different experiences affect how easily young children learn to deal with feelings. Among these factors are birth order, and hospitalization, trauma, or separation from the primary caregiver.

Birth order. Often a child 12 to 24 months old picks up information about feelings while a parent is trying to teach an older sibling.

Hospitalization, trauma, and separation. In general, young children who have been hospitalized or experienced trauma or separations from their parents have more difficulty learning to cope with their feelings than other children do. The parental separation can be due to illness, neglect, work, or travel.

Parental modeling. Parents can facilitate kids' learning to deal with disappointment by being sensitive to their children's feelings and open about their own feelings and coping strategies. When parents verbalize their feelings and the ways they deal with feelings and situations, children can observe a variety of tools in use. This modeling makes it easier for children to learn about feelings.

ℐ♥ *Questions and answers*

This approach of teaching skills seems like a lot of work. Is it really necessary?

Yes and no. Many children learn to deal with feelings without intentional teaching, and others don't. If your child learns to deal with his feelings, then teaching is not necessary. On the other hand, if your child has trouble dealing with disappointment, frustration, or anger and you wish your child to have the benefits of being emotionally competent, you, or someone, will need to take the time to teach him how to deal with his feelings.

I tried to teach my daughter to calm herself but it didn't work. What's wrong?

Usually when a person has trouble, he or she has rushed the teaching process by skipping a step. Sometimes you can get away with that, other times you can't. The step parents most commonly skip is "practicing the tool in pretend."

Most of the time, children need to practice a skill many times before they can use it for real. Just as watching French movies to get an "ear" for the language before you go to France helps, the more familiar your child is with a tool, the more easily she will be able to recall the language or skill when she needs it.

Review of how to teach self-calming tools

1. Introduce the tool.
2. Link the tool to feeling calm.
3. Practice using the tool in pretend.
4. Prompt the child to use the tool
5. Back out and let the child act independently.

I was never taught to deal with my feelings and sometimes have trouble with anger. How am I going to teach my child?

Fortunately, you do not need to be perfect to help your children deal with their feelings. You can take an anger management class or learn as you teach feelings tools to your child. One woman who had a volatile temper asked her four-year-old son to help her remember to take deep breaths when she got upset. By helping his mother, her son learned to associate breathing with calming oneself and began to use it to calm himself.

I read that boys' brains have more testosterone than girls', and that is why they're so aggressive. Isn't it wrong to teach them to be different from what they are?

It is true that most boys' brains have more testosterone than girls' brains, and because of that many (not all) are physically restless or intense. Even so, it is the parents' job to teach their children the acceptable ways to express feelings or restless energy in their culture. In the United States, that means expressing one's anger respectfully rather than physically. Parents will need to teach boys ways to dissipate physical tension, usually through movement. Walk with boys while you talk to them so they can think better. Many men also like to pace while they think.

I would like to help my child, but I didn't learn much about feelings as a child. What can I do?

It is difficult to teach your child information you did not receive. There are two ways you can approach the problem. One is to find a mentor. The mentor could be a friend, parent educator, counselor, therapist – someone who is comfortable with children's feelings. When you are confused or concerned you can ask your mentor for help. Another way is to enroll in a class on feelings, either through an anger management or a parent education class. In either case, you will need to adapt the material you learn for use with your particular child.

When should I start teaching "feeling skills?"

You can begin teaching about feelings any time. You can inventory the skills your child needs and start with what is missing or look at your child's developmental level and start with what she is able to learn now. For example, when your child is a baby comfort him and explain what you are doing. "You are crying. What's the matter? You're not wet and you just ate. Are you lonely? I'll pick you up. Do you feel better now?" To a toddler, you can offer choices. "You are mad that I won't give you a cookie now. Would you like to cry or shake out the mads?"

With a preschooler or school-aged child, you can acknowledge the feelings and provide a structure. "You are really upset that your friend can't come over, and it's not okay to hurt your sister. What else can you do with your frustration?" With school-aged children and teens, you can reflect their feelings and let them know you are there for them without offering information or advice. If a child seems unable to function on an appropriate level, then look at the "Skills inventory" on page 28 and see what he or she needs, or seek outside help.

How do I know if my child needs help?

It is sometimes hard to know if your child's temperament makes him or her slow to pick up feelings information, or if there is some underlying cause that is preventing your child from learning to manage his or her feelings. These five questions may help you decide.

Has your child always been intense? Was she intense as a baby, a toddler, a preschooler? If she was, you may be dealing with a temperament issue. She will need consistent support and direction over time.

If you can pinpoint a time when the anger or particular feelings started, review the events in the child's life around that time for possible causes. Some common issues are: separation from the primary caregiver, hospitalization, physical or emotional trauma, birth of a sibling, changes in household structure. When these things happen, children often develop unresolved anger that needs to be addressed before they can deal with current feelings or events.

Is the behavior typical for the child's age? For example, temper tantrums are typical for two-year-olds. Power struggles are typical for four-year-olds. However, if you have a six-year-old who gets angry at the slightest thing or throws himself around like a toddler, that is not typical.

Is the behavior getting better? For some children, learning to recognize and deal with their feelings takes a long time. However, if the child is learning, life should be getting calmer. You can make notes on a calendar or in a notebook to record the length and intensity of the outbursts. That way you can look back and notice if things are getting better or not.

Have you carried out a well-thought-out plan? Sometimes parents hope their child will outgrow the volatile behavior, so they try to be flexible and avoid confrontations. With some children this may work, but with most you are simply postponing the problem. If you have tried the approach in this book for several months with no change, then your child may need additional help.

Does your intuition or gut tell you that something is wrong? Has a relative or caregiver who works with your child mentioned any concerns? Have you a sense that something is not as it should be? Follow your intuition.

If you are still unsure after answering these questions, find a professional (doctor, school counselor, child psychologist, therapist) and ask for advice. Help and support are available; sometimes you have to look for them.

Closing

Congratulations on persevering this far in this book. You are well on your way to helping your child deal with the ups and downs of life. Remember that a child's success and happiness in life are more dependent on his emotional sensitivity and resilience than on his intelligence or formal training.

Your job is to offer information and support and then to gradually back off. You begin with direct support as the nurturer, then teach skills by offering choices. Next, coach children by providing structure. Finally, back out and take the role of consultant, responding when they wish your help.

The transition from emotional dependence to independence is rarely smooth. However, with time you can help your child deal with disappointment and other strong feelings. As the ancient sage said, "Happiness is not a destination, it is a mode of travel."

Best wishes for the remainder of your journey!

Appendix A

The cost of emotional illiteracy

When children do not have the ability to soothe themselves, resolve their problems, and understand others' feelings, they are vulnerable to a host of problems. Here we will look briefly at five: academic trouble, aggression, alcohol and drug addiction, depression, and eating disorders.

Academic trouble. It has been known for a long time that high IQ alone does not adequately predict success as an adult. Daniel Goleman, author of *Emotional Intelligence,* describes the structure and circuitry of the brain, how thought and feeling are interwoven, and how emotional distress can reduce intellectual ability.

> He remarks, "The prefrontal cortex is the brain region responsible for working memory. But circuits from the limbic brain [emotional brain] to the prefrontal lobes mean that the signals of strong emotion – anxiety, anger, and the like – can create neural static, sabotaging the ability of the prefrontal lobes to maintain working memory. That is why when we are emotionally upset we say we "just can't think straight" – and why continual emotional distress can create deficits in a child's intellectual abilities, crippling the capacity to learn."

Goleman goes on to describe a study of primary school boys with above average IQ who were doing poorly in school. The study found the boys to have impaired frontal cortex functioning. They were also impulsive and anxious, often in trouble. "Despite their intellectual potential these are the children at highest risk for academic failure, alcoholism, and criminality – not because their intellect was deficient, but because their control over their emotional life was impaired."

This ability of poor emotional functioning to overshadow thought processes can explain why some people with tremendous potential do not accomplish much.

Aggression. One trait common to angry, aggressive children is that they perceive slights where none were intended, and imagine peers to be more hostile toward them than they actually are. This leads them to misinterpret neutral acts as threatening and to retaliate.

This jump to judgement shows a deeply rooted perceptual bias in people who are unusually aggressive. They jump to action on the basis of an assumed threat and pay little attention to what is actually happening. The more children do this, the more automatic their aggression becomes. These children are emotionally vulnerable, in that they have limited capacity for upset, getting more upset at more things than other children.

Goleman reports that studies following such children from preschool years into their teens have found that "half of the first graders who are disruptive, unable to get along with other kids, disobedient with their parents, and resistant with teachers will become delinquents in their teen years." He adds that, of course, not all of these children are on a path to violence and crime, but they are more at risk.

Drug and alcohol addiction. By the time teens graduate from high school, 90% have tried alcohol, but only 14% go on to become alcoholics. Those students most vulnerable to alcohol or drug addiction seem to find in the alcohol or drug an instant way to soothe emotions that have distressed them. Goleman sites a study that tracked several hundred seventh- and eighth-grade students for two years. The students reporting the highest level of emotional distress or anger went on to have the highest rate of substance abuse.

Depression. Childhood depression, once unheard of, is on the rise. Some epidemiological studies have found that for boys and girls between 10 and 13 the rate is as high as 8 or 9 percent. Goleman notes that what has recently emerged is that children who are most prone to despondency tend toward a pessimistic outlook even before they become depressed. Further, that with training and support children can learn the skills to reverse depression.

Eating disorders. Gloria Leone, a University of Minnesota psychologist who studies eating disorders, has observed that among young girls, those who have a poor awareness of their feelings and their body signals have the strongest likelihood of developing an eating disorder over the next two years. When they are upset or have trouble with a friend, these girls cannot distinguish between anger, anxiety, or hunger. All sensations are lumped together. They often turn to food as a way to soothe themselves. This in turn can become an eating disorder when accompanied by a desire to be thin.

We have looked at five potential outcomes of emotional illiteracy. The solution is not for the parent or teacher to make these children's lives emotionally smooth, but to give these children the skills they need to choose happiness and emotional competence.

Appendix B

Activities for understanding feelings

Children need to understand the nature of feelings to develop emotional competence. The activities in this appendix can help children develop a vocabulary, notice feelings inside, separate feelings from actions, recognize that feelings change, and understand how different people feel and respond differently.

Develop vocabulary, page 101	Read Books; Feeling Search; Mirror Feelings; Speak Up
Identify feelings, page 103	Point to Feeling; 1-10, How Big?; Describe Your Feelings; How Does Mad Feel Inside?
Understand feelings change, page 105	Twist the Dial; Bedtime Review, Elf Card Stories, Story Talk
Separate feelings and actions, page 107	Action List; Stop the Story; Inside-Outside; Reporter
Identify choices, page 109	Read "Choice" Books; Draw Four; Puppet Choices; Stop the Video
Know other people have feelings, page 111	I Like Vanilla. What Do You Like?; Charades; Feelings Hunt; Detective

✐ Develop vocabulary

The first step in understanding feelings is to develop a feelings vocabulary. The easiest way for children to learn is in context. The parent can name the child's feeling or his or her own feeling. However, some parents are more comfortable introducing feeling words to children with books or activities.

Children need names for a wide variety of feelings. They need words for both comfortable and uncomfortable feelings and for mild and intense feelings.

Read Books

Purpose: To increase vocabulary by reading books.

Materials: Books that illustrate feelings. Examples are listed in Appendix E.

Directions: You can use books in several ways:
- Sit with the child in a comfortable place and read the book.
- Cover up the word and ask the child to guess the emotion by looking at the pictures. *"How do you think that child feels?"*
- Look at a picture that shows a feeling and talk about a time you felt that way.

Tips:
- Be willing to read the books many times.
- Keep the tone fun rather than serious or "educational."

Feeling Search

Purpose: To increase a feelings vocabulary by looking for people exhibiting feelings.

Materials: None

Directions: Go someplace where people often display feelings – the mall, a park, or a sporting event. Watch for feelings.

A man slumped over on a bench might feel sad or dejected.

A child trying to build a sand castle might be frustrated or angry.
Comment on what you see and how you think the person might feel.

Tips:
- Keep your observations uncritical. Change "The naughty boy is having a tantrum" to "The boy is mad. He has to wait for his turn on the slide."
- Make a list of feelings you want to introduce to your child and look for examples of them.

Mirror Feelings

Purpose: To teach children a vocabulary by reflecting their feelings.

Materials: None

Directions: Reflect your child's feelings. Include both the feeling and the cause or context of the feeling.

"You're mad that you may not watch another video today."
Or, *"You look content curled up on the couch with your book."*
Reflect a variety of feelings – both pleasant and unpleasant, and intense and mild.

Tips:
- Log the feelings words you use in a day. Compare the number of words for pleasant and uncomfortable feelings.
- Pick particular feelings you wish to introduce and look for examples of them.

Speak Up

Purpose: To teach children a vocabulary by labeling your feelings.

Materials: None

Directions: Tune into your own feelings. Share them with your child. Include both the feeling and the cause of the feeling. For example, *"I'm frustrated that I can't get the checkbook to balance." "I'm pleased at how the cake turned out."* Or in the car, *"I'm mad that man cut me off."* Use a variety of words.

ℐ Identify feelings

Children sometimes feel overwhelmed by their feelings. They need to be able to identify feelings in real situations, otherwise a vocabulary does them little good. When you identify feelings, children learn both a feelings vocabulary and that feelings are normal.

Point to Feelings

Purpose: To help children identify their feelings by pointing to a picture of their feeling.

Materials: A book or poster on feelings. See list in Appendix E.

Directions: Look at a book or chart with your child. Say, *"Point to how you feel."* Acknowledge whatever feeling the child points to. For example, *"Oh, you're feeling sad."*

Tips:
- Ask in a gentle, mildly curious tone.
- If the child is verbal, you can add, *"Would you like to talk about it?"* If the child says, *"No"* you can reply, *"I'll be here if you want to talk."*

Note: Many children are able to point to a picture that illustrates their feelings when they can't verbalize the word. This is true for toddlers and for teens.

1 to 10, How Big?

Purpose: To help children figure out how upset they are, using a scale of 1 to 10.

Materials: None

Directions:

1. Introduce the concept by describing something that happened to you.
   "Today at work Mr. Smith blamed me for spilling coffee on his report. I was angry he thought I could be that careless. On a scale of 1 to 10, I was '6,' mad."
2. Reflect on a previous situation.
   "Remember when Billy broke your airplane? How mad were you on a scale of 1 to 10 when 1 is not very mad and 10 is terribly mad?"
3. Apply to a current situation with the child.

Tips:

- Acknowledge the child's feelings before you ask the child how intense they are. A ten on the scale can be either the best or worst thing a child has experienced, whichever works for your child.

- Talk in a gentle, nonjudgmental tone.

Comment: Children sometimes feel overwhelmed by their feelings. When you label their feelings, children learn feelings are okay.

Describe Your Feelings

Purpose: To give children permission to consider their feelings by modeling describing your feelings.

Materials: None

Directions: When you share your feelings, include both your feelings and the context. For example: *"I'm so excited. My sister is coming tomorrow and I haven't seen her for ages."* Or, *"I am really frustrated. All I want to do is write a simple letter, and my computer keeps crashing."*

Tips:

- Reflect both pleasant feelings and uncomfortable feelings.
- *Caution:* Choose situations that do not involve your children. If you focus on your feelings in relation to your children's actions, your children may incorrectly assume they are responsible for your feelings.
- Describing your feelings also helps increase your child's vocabulary.

How Does Mad Feel Inside?

Purpose: To help children identify their emotions by focusing on the feelings inside their bodies.

Materials: None

Directions: Begin by talking about how your emotions feel inside (physically). For example, after you have just missed being hit by another car you might say, *"I am so scared. My heart is beating fast. My body feels so heavy I can hardly move."* Or at the park on a beautiful day, you might say, *"I feel contented. I feel warm and bright and calm inside."*

Then you can ask your child to describe what he feels like inside. Is he warm or cool, heavy or light, tight or loose, etc.?

✐ *Understand feelings change*

Children live in the present. They believe they will always feel as they feel right now. When a friend is mad at them now, many children feel their friend will always be mad at them.

When children understand that feelings change (both their own and other peoples'), it is easier for them to control their feelings. Many parents and caregivers are tempted to tell kids, *"Relax. You will feel better tomorrow."* However, that rarely works. Most children need to learn for themselves.

Twist the Feelings Dial

Purpose: To help children notice that feelings change using a feelings dial.

Materials: Scissors, marking pens, and one set of these materials for each person: a paper plate, a strip of cardboard or heavy paper about ½ inch by 3 inches long, and a small metal fastener or paper clip.

Directions:

1. *Make the feelings dial.* Divide the paper plate into four or more sections. Draw a simple feeling face in each section. Cut a point on one end of the strip of cardboard to form a "pointer." Using the fastener, poke a hole in the center of the plate. Poke the fastener into the flat end of the cardboard pointer and then into the hole in the plate. Now you have a feelings dial. Make one feelings dial for each person.

2. *Dial a feeling.* Aim the pointer towards your feeling. Then ask your child to aim the pointer on her dial to her feeling. Tell her that when her feeling changes she can move the pointer again. Later, when your feelings change, take your feelings dial to the child and say, *"Now I feel _____"* and move the pointer to the new feeling.

3. *Reflect on change.* Later talk about all the times feelings change during the morning or the day.

Tips:
- Add more feelings words as you need them.
- Set the dial when you or your child leaves the house. Check it when you or your child returns. Talk about feeling changes that happened while you were gone.

Bedtime Review

Purpose: To help children notice that feelings change by remembering all the things (pleasant and unpleasant) that happened that day.

Materials: None

Directions: At bedtime settle yourself and your child comfortably. Then take a mental walk through the day, remembering the events and feelings. For example, you might say the following to a toddler.

> *When you got up this morning, you felt happy the sun was shining. After breakfast we went to the park. You were excited to climb on the new slide. When you wanted to swing, all the swings were full and you were disappointed and cried. Soon someone got off and you were happy again.*

Variations: It is easier for very young children to point rather than speak. You can draw feelings on your finger tips: happy, mad, silly, scared, sad. Ask your child to point to the feelings she had during the day.

Tips:
- Keep the tone light and pleasant.
- Include a variety of feelings, both comfortable and uncomfortable.
- If something scary or infuriating happened, review how the child solved the problem and/or ask him what he would try if it happened again.
- Resist the temptation to tell the child what he did wrong and what he should do next time.

Elf Card Stories

Purpose: To help children notice that feelings change by making up stories about changing feelings.

Materials: A deck of feelings cards. You can purchase a set of colorful *Feeling Elf Cards* from Parenting Press (see Appendix E) or make a set of feelings cards by writing feelings words on 3x5 cards.

Directions: Ask your child to choose or draw three (or more) elf cards that display different feelings. Then you make up a story about an elf that relates to those feelings. You can be as elaborate or succinct as you wish.

For example, if you drew curious, scared, furious, and pleased cards, you could tell the following story:

> *An elf was playing in the zoo. She saw an open door and was very curious where it went. When she stepped inside, she saw a lion, felt scared and froze. The lion roared at her. That made her furious, so she stomped out and slammed the door. When she thought about what happened, she was pleased the lion roared and didn't try to eat her.*

Variations:

• Parent and children take turns making up the story.
• Draw one or two elf cards and share a story about when you felt those feelings.

Story Talk

Purpose: To help children notice that feelings change by making up stories about changing feelings.

Materials: Books in which the character changes feelings

For example, *All My Feelings At Home: Ellie's Day* and *All My Feelings At Preschool: Nathan's Day*. See Appendix E for references.

Directions: At the end of each page (or when the character's feeling changes) ask, "How does _____ (the character) feel?" "Why does he (she) feel that way?" "What can he (she) do about the feeling?"

Tip: Keep your tone light and curious, rather than serious, judgmental, or educational.

Variations:

• Use the feelings dial from "Twist the Feelings Dial" to indicate when the character's feelings change.
• Make a list of the character's feelings on a piece of paper. Review all the feelings when you are done reading the story.
• Talk about what alternative responses the character might make.

✐ Separate feelings from actions

Feelings are on the inside. Actions are on the outside. All feelings are okay. Some actions are okay, others are not okay. For example, it is okay to feel angry, and it is not okay to hit someone. Children need to learn the difference between feelings and actions.

Actions List

Purpose: To help children understand that feelings are different from actions by making and posting a list of acceptable actions.

Materials: A large piece of paper and markers

Directions: Describe the difference between feelings and behavior. For example, *"Feelings are on the inside. Actions are on the outside. All feelings are okay. Some actions are okay, others are not. It is okay to feel angry, and it is not okay to hit someone."*

Explain that together you are going to make a list of things she can do when she is upset. If the child cannot read, draw pictures of the ideas. Ask her to decorate the list. Then hang it on the refrigerator or somewhere she can find it easily. A list might include: ask for a hug, cry in my room, curl up in the sun like a cat, and take a deep breath.

Tips:
• Observe your child and notice ways she calms herself down.
• Review self-calming tools in Chapter 4 or Appendix C for ideas.

Stop the Story

Purpose: To help children understand that feelings are different from actions by separating a story character's feelings and actions.

Materials: Book or video

Directions: Sit down with your child and start to read. When the main character does something, stop reading and ask, *"What was _____(the character) feeling? What did he (she) do?"* If your child can't answer, ask, *"How would you feel?"* If your child still can't (or won't) respond, you can say, *"Well, I think the character might feel . . . "*

Variation: Watch a video with your child. Stop the video and ask the questions above.

Inside-Outside

Purpose: To help children understand that feelings are different from actions by using scarves to act out a situation.

Materials: A scarf for each person and a list of situations

Directions: Choose a situation and read it out loud. Squat down and cover yourself with a scarves. Say, *"Inside I feel . . ."* Then take off the scarf, stand up and say, *"Outside I feel . . ."* For example, the situation was *"A large black dog is barking at you."* You might cover yourself and say *"I feel very scared inside."* Then stand, take off the scarf, and say, *"I will take a deep breath and walk slowly."*

Situation ideas

- A large black dog is barking at you.
- Someone grabs your toy/hat.
- You get a present you really, really wanted.
- Your friend invites you camping.
- Dad says you may not go camping with your friend.
- Your friend says, "I don't like you."
- You may not watch the new cool television show.
- You are the last person picked for soccer team.
- You are having broccoli (or a vegetable you hate) for supper.
- You've just learned to tie a shoe/ride a bike/read/climb a tree, etc.

Tip: Focus on the difference between the feeling and event, not on what the child "should" or "could" do.

Variations:
- Make up your own situations. Consider including situations your child has experienced.
- Write each situation on a slip of paper or 3x5 card. Let the child choose a situation to act out.
- Play the game without scarves.

Reporter

Purpose: To help children understand that feelings are different from actions by asking people how they felt in specific situations (past or present).

Materials: Paper and pencil (or a tape recorder) to take notes (optional)

Directions: For example, if a ladder fell over and hit Uncle Ben on the head, a child could ask, *"How did you feel when the ladder hit you?"* and *"What did you do?"* Uncle Ben might reply, *"At first, I was scared and then I felt stupid for leaving the ladder where it was unstable."* Then he might add, *"The first thing I did was to touch my head to tell if it was bleeding. Then I called for help since I wasn't sure I should move since I blacked out for a moment."*

Tip: Ask questions about a variety of feelings – happy, excited, bored, frustrated, angry, etc.

✐ *Identify choices*

Children always have choices for what they can do in a situation. To begin with they can focus on their feelings – identify them and calm themselves. Or, they can focus on the situation – decide what is the problem and look for various ways to respond. Some choices are more constructive than others. When you list ideas, record both constructive and unconstructive ideas. You want your child to learn how to distinguish between them.

Read "Choice" Books

Purpose: To introduce a variety of choices for a situation.

Materials: I'm Mad, I Want It, or the "choice" books listed in Appendix E.

Directions: Read the story. When the main characters come to a decision, let your child choose what the character does. Turn to the appropriate page and continue reading. After you find out what the character did, ask your child, *"How did you like that choice? What else could she have done?"* Your child can follow another path through the book.

Tip: Do not get upset if your child chooses a "bad" choice. The purpose of the books is to help children think about the consequences of different decisions without having to experience the consequences for themselves.

Draw Four

Purpose: To help children think of alternatives by drawing pictures.

Materials: Large piece of paper and marking pens

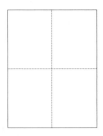

Directions: Fold the paper in half and then in half again, so it has four sections. Describe a situation and ask your child to draw one thing he could do in each section of the paper. When he is done, acknowledge his effort, *"Wow, you thought of four ways to handle that problem."* If the situation is one that recurs, suggest he post the picture on the refrigerator so he will have the ideas when he needs them again.

Tips:
• Do not evaluate the ideas. Evaluation stops the creative flow. The goal is first to think of different ideas, and second, to think of good ideas.
• If your child has trouble thinking of things he could do, ask him what he would do if he was a magician, Superman, the President, or the character from his favorite story.

Puppet Choices

Purpose: To introduce a variety of choices for a situation with the use of puppets.

Materials: Puppets

Directions: Choose a situation for the puppets to act out. It can be something the child is facing or a story (for example, *I Want It* by Elizabeth Crary). Introduce the characters and story.

When the characters have a problem, stop the action and turn to your child and say, "_____ (character) has a problem. What could he do?" Give your child time to think. If he says, "I don't know," offer two ideas and ask, "What could the puppet try first?"

When you are finished, ask how he liked the ending. Ask what the puppet might do differently next time.

Tip: Do not push a particular idea. When adults push a particular idea, children may conclude it is the *only* right answer. It is more important for the child to learn *how to think* of good ideas rather than to remember a correct answer for a specific situation.

Stop the Video

Purpose: To help children think of a variety of ideas and to realize that there are many possibilities even for stories.

Materials: A story or video. Pad of paper and pencil (optional)

Directions: Sit with the child to read the book or watch the video. Occasionally stop the story and ask, "What else could he (the character) do?" You can jot down your child's ideas. If all the ideas are similar, ask your child to think of a different idea. For example, you might say, "Hitting and pushing are hurting ideas. What is a different idea?" Then return to the story. Repeat a couple of times during the story.

Tip: Stop the story when the character is doing both "good" and "bad" things. That way the child will learn that you always have a variety of choices.

✐ *Know that other people have feelings*

Young children are egocentric. They often believe either that no one else has feelings or that their feelings are more important than other people's. Children will be more successful getting what they want and dealing with their feelings if they realize that others have feelings, too.

I Like Vanilla. What Do You Like?

Purpose: To help children realize that other people (adults and children) have feelings, and those feelings may be different from their feelings.

Materials: Several children, preferably five or more. Pictures or list of different things (optional).

Directions: The adult or one of the children picks an item and asks, "Who likes _____ best?" For example, one might ask, *"Who likes strawberry ice cream more than vanilla ice cream?"* Or, *"Who like dogs more than cats?"* As the adult, observe the differences and comment on them. *"Interesting, half the kids prefer strawberry ice cream rather than vanilla."* The play rotates to another child who asks, *"Who likes . . . ?"*

Note: When children know that people feel differently, negotiation is easier.

Charades

Purpose: To help children identify what a person is feeling.

Number of players: Three or more

Materials: A stack of feelings words or pictures of people showing emotions.

Directions: One person draws a word and thinks of a time when she felt that way. Then she acts out the feeling – using facial expressions and body motions to convey the feeling. Other people guess the feeling. When someone guesses correctly, a new person chooses a card and acts the feeling. When everyone has had a chance to act a feeling, shuffle the cards and start over again.

Feelings Hunt

Purpose: To help children notice what another person is feeling

Materials:
• Paper or 3x5 cards for feelings pictures or words
• A copy of *The Way I Feel* by Janan Cain or another book that illustrates feelings (optional)

Directions: Go to the mall, park, or ball game – somewhere where people show feelings. List the feelings that someone might feel, one feeling per card. For example, happy, tired, angry, excited, frustrated, content. If children are young, collect pictures of people showing the feelings. Spread the cards out where your child can see them. Ask her to help you find examples of those feelings in the people you watch. When you recognize a feeling, ask, "Why do you think he feels _____?"

Note: If your child gets restless or bored, change to another game. Little good will be accomplished by forcing the play.

Detective – How Do You Feel Now?

Purpose: To help children identify what a person is feeling and learn four ways to get information.

Materials: People to observe

A notebook for notes (optional). A copy of *The Way I Feel* by Janan Cain or another book that illustrates feelings (optional).

Directions: Tell your child you are going to play detective and that it is her job to discover how people feel.

Explain that there are four ways she can tell how a person feels: (1) what he looks like, (2) what he sounds like, (3) what he feels like if you touch him and (4) what he says if you ask him how he feels.

Let her observe someone (like a sibling). Ask her to notice how the person looks, sounds, and moves. If she can't determine what the other person is feeling, suggest she use the last tool – ask him.

Observe several people or the same person several different times.

Tip: Start with people who are willing to be observed.

Tools for coping with feelings

Children need a variety of ways to calm or comfort themselves. Different tools work better for different children, and some tools are appropriate in different settings.

   This section has six groups of tools. Each group has four different tools. Each individual tool has an example of how this tool worked with a child, some comments on the tool in general, and several ways to teach the tool. You can scan the sections to find tools that appeal to you. You can also try something "wild" and see how that works.

Physical tools, Page 114	Large Movements; Shake Off the Feelings; Breathe in Calmness; Hold Yourself Together
Auditory/verbal tools, Page 115	Talk to Someone; Use Positive Self-talk; Listen to Music; Sing a Silly Song
Visual tools, Page 117	Read a Book; Look Outside; Visualize a Calm Place; Watch the Aquarium
Creative tools, Page 118	Draw a Picture; Write a Letter; Make Something; Bake Bread
Self-calming tools, Page 120	Get a Hug; Drink from a Water Bottle; Take a Warm Bath; Get a Snack
Humor tools, Page 121	Read Humor Books; Watch Funny Videos; Find Humor in the Situation; Make Silly Faces

ℐ *Physical tools*

Large Movements

Paul is very physical. When he was little, he would hit someone when he was upset. Now when he is angry with his sister, he goes in the hall and jogs in place until he's calm.

Large rhythmic movements – running, dancing, swimming – reduce anger and frustration. Short motions, like hitting a pillow, have no effect or increase anger. For some kids hiking in the woods is very helpful.

How to teach:
- Model movement when you are upset. Afterward mention how calm you feel.
- Make a mad dance. When your child is calm, create a silly dance.
- When your child is upset, offer her the choice of running or dancing a mad dance with you.
- Invite your child to dance (or run) with you when you are mad.

Shake Off the Feelings

At the beginning of the school year, Zack solved all problems by pushing or hitting. The problem has almost disappeared. Yesterday, I say him shaking his hands vigorously. I asked him what he was doing. He said, "I shake out mads."

Repetitive movement (like shaking or knitting or wiggling a foot) often has a calming effect on people. It's as though some of the negative energy gets used up.

How to teach:
- Model "shaking out mads." When the serviceman phones to say you need to wait another week for the part to come, you can say, "I'm so mad I feel like screaming, but I'm going to 'shake out the mads'" and then shake vigorously.
- When your child is calm, have him pretend to "shake out mads."

Breathe in Calmness

Yesterday when Adam knocked Allie's tower over, she started to hit him, then stopped, closed her eyes, and took a long slow breath. I'm so proud. We've been working on this for a long time.

Deep breathing is a classic way to calm feelings and refocus. To be effective, the breath should expand the abdomen.

How to teach:
- Show your child how to focus on his breath by blowing out a candle.
- Teach your child to take deep breaths. Fold a file card in half to make

a tent. Then take a deep breath and slowly blow the card across the table.
- Teach your child tummy breathing. Ask him to lie down, and to notice if his chest or his tummy move as he breathes. Tell him when you see his tummy moving.

Hold Yourself Together

Joel was having trouble in school. When he was upset he would "fall apart" and cry or flail. We taught him to put his arms around himself to "hold himself together" and to avoid hitting someone else.

For some people, firm pressure inward on their bodies is very comforting. The sensation may be similar to that achieved by the "swaddling" that some cultures do to calm their babies.

How to teach:
- Model "holding yourself together" when you are agitated. To do that: Cross your arms. Put your hands on your shoulders. Pull inward, toward the center of your body. (See above.)
- "Hold your child together" when he begins to get upset. The pressure needs to be firm – not light or hard.
- Give your child a blanket in which to wrap up to create pressure all over.
- Play "holding yourself together" with your child.

ℐ⌐ *Auditory/verbal tools*

Talk to Someone

Yesterday Marian came rushing over to me, crying, "Danny tore Curious George!" Instead of telling her he didn't mean it or offering to tape it, I pulled her onto my lap and just listened. In a minute or two she hopped off and went back to playing.

Often being listened to helps people feel heard, then move on.

How to teach:
- Stop what you are doing and give your entire attention to your child.
- Gently reflect the feelings you hear.
- Avoid the temptation to give advice or "fix" the situation.
- Model talking about your feelings. *"That was Marty on the phone. She can't come over tomorrow. I am disappointed, I was really looking forward to seeing her."*

Use Positive Self-talk

When Brianna was young, she got frustrated very easily. She would end up saying, "I'm stupid! I can't do anything." We taught her to change her self-talk. Now when she is upset she says, "Learning takes time. I can learn even when I feel frustrated."

Self-talk strongly colors the mind. It impacts what we feel, see, and do.

How to teach:
- Model positive self-talk. If someone was rude to you, you could say, "*I am in charge of my feelings. I will take a deep breath and then decide what to do.*"
- Give affirming messages. "*It is okay to be angry.*" "*You can be upset and still think what to do.*"
- Model changing negative self-talk. When you say something negative, say, "*Oops,*" and change it to something positive.

Listen to Music

When my boys are getting too wound up, I will put on a Sousa march to get their attention and then gradually change to quieter music. This will help them calm down.

Music can be used to influence feelings. You have experienced this when you watch television or a movie. You can use music to help your child cope with feelings.

How to teach:
- Notice how your child reacts to music. Some kids get wound up; others relax.
- Talk about how music makes you feel. Sad when you hear _____. Cheerful when you hear _____. Lonely when you hear _____.
- Listen to music with your child, ask how he feels when he hears the music. When your child is upset or very happy, ask what music he would like to hear.

Sing a Silly Song

When Chris was about 17 months old, he hated having his diaper changed. One day when he was fighting it more actively than usual, I remarked, "You're mad." He stopped kicking, got a quizzical look on his face, then started shaking his hands and blowing air out. He was applying the song "When you're mad and you know it . . . " we had been singing for three months.

Song is stored in the same part of the brain as feelings. When you sing information about feelings, it is more easily accessible to children.

How to teach:
- Model singing to yourself. When you are upset or happy, sing a song.
- Sing *"When You're Mad and You Know It"* by Elizabeth Crary and Shari Steelsmith. Words are in Appendix D.
- Sing *"I whistle a happy tune"* from "The King and I."
- Make up silly songs and act them out. For example, *"You are mad, are you not? You can cry or you can hop."*

ℐ⌐ *Visual tools*

Read a Book

I can tell when Erin has had a tough day at school. After she puts her stuff away, she grabs a book and retreats to a corner to read. Half an hour later she stops and is ready for a snack. If I try to talk with her before then, she disintegrates.

For many people, reading a book helps them calm themselves. Reading is enjoyable and gives them a focus.

How to teach:
- Model the tool. When you have an argument with a friend, you can say, *"I'm so mad I need to calm down. I'm going to read for a little bit and then decide what to do."* When you're done say, *"That felt good. I feel calmer now."*
- When your child is upset, say, *"You look frustrated with the puzzle. Would it help you calm down if I read you a story?"*

Look Outside

Carol started wearing glasses when very young. Other kids' teasing really bothered her. When she cried, they teased her more. She learned to detach from the situation by looking as far away as she could. Eventually she became so calm they stopped teasing.

When feelings are running high, it is often helpful to detach from the situation. One way to do that is to look outside. Watch the trees (if any) or the clouds or focus on the farthest thing you can see.

How to teach:
- Model looking outside to calm yourself. Say, *"I'm too upset to think. I'll look out the window to calm myself."* Comment on what you see and when calm, say, *"I feel calmer now."*
- Make a game of looking out the window. You might say, *"I spy something red."* Or, *"What do the clouds remind you of?"*

Visualize a Calm Place

My son, Ben, is now ignoring taunts from his older brother. I asked Ben what he was doing differently. He said, "I go to the beach in my mind." When I looked puzzled, he added, "I see the sand. I feel the sun. I listen to the waves. And then his words don't bother me."

A calm place can be a place you have visited, a cozy bed, or rocking in Grandma's lap.

How to teach:
- Store up calm feelings. Go to the park and talk about how calm and soothing it feels. Say, *"We can store these feelings and use them when we get frustrated."*
- Use the feelings in pretend. When she is having fun, say, *"Let's pretend we're angry and call back the calm feelings."* Model recalling the calm feelings.
- When she begins to get frustrated, ask, "Would you like to get the calm feelings back?"

Watch the Aquarium

John has watched fish to calm himself since he was an infant. His crib was next to an aquarium as a baby. When he was fussy, we would put him in his crib facing the fish. Within a couple of minutes he was calm.

Some people find watching gentle repetitive movement calming. Watching fish swim, trees sway, or a lava lamp bubble are soothing.

How to teach:
- When you are in a relaxed mode, sit with your child on your lap and watch the fish. Let your feelings drain out. Remark on how restful it is to watch the fish.
- When your child is restless ask, *"Would you like to watch the fish with me? "*
- Watch your child. Notice if she is intrigued by things she sees. If she is more interested in running or talking, this tool may be less effective.

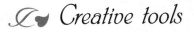 *Creative tools*

Draw a Picture

In my family, drawing was encouraged as an expression for feelings. I can remember as a child watching my brother break four pencil points drawing a picture of how angry he was.

Drawing can be an excellent way to release feelings. The person can focus on drawing his feelings or what he would like to do.

How to teach:
- When you are upset, sit down and draw (or scribble) how you feel. Talk about why you feel like that.
- Provide colored markers or crayons. Scribble a large red patch on your

paper. Ask, "*How do you feel when you see lots of red?*" Ask, "*Which colors make you feel happy?*"

• When your child is upset, suggest he draw a picture of how he feels.

Write a Letter

I remember as a child being livid with my father. He dropped me at my grandmother's and left before I was able to figure out why I was so mad. That night I poured out my feelings in a letter. When I was done, I felt much better. It is a technique I still use today.

Writing a letter can be a wonderful way to let go of feelings, particularly if you leave it 24 hours and reread it before sending it. This idea can be expanded to writing in a journal or diary.

How to teach:

• Model writing your feelings in a letter. Say, "*I am angry with the way the clerk treated me today. I am going to write a letter about how I felt.*"

• Link to a situation. Ask, "*Remember when you were mad at Martin this morning? What would you have liked to tell him?*"

• Say, "*You sound very angry about that. Would you like to write your teacher a letter?*"

Make Something

My daughter likes to make beaded jewelry. We noticed that when she is upset with school or her brother, she will busy herself making a bracelet. By the time she is done, all her irritation is gone.

When people are upset, they often have a restless energy. Many people find a repetitive activity they enjoy reduces the stress.

How to teach:

• Model making something to reduce stress. For example, making squares for a quilt, folding origami, or carving wooden animals. Talk about how making quilt pieces helps you to get calm.

• Reflect how calm your child appears when she is making something.

• Invite the child to help you make something. For example, when the dog dies, invite your child to help sort photos to make a scrap book. Talk about how making the scrapbook eases your feelings.

Bake Bread

One day my son came come from school in a foul mood. He was taking out his frustration on his sister. In an attempt to distract him I asked him to help me knead bread, which he did. The change was dramatic.

Kneading bread can be very soothing. The movement is repetitive. The dough is slightly warm. And the smell when it bakes is wonderful.

How to teach:
- Model the tool. When you are upset you can say, *"I'm so frustrated I need to calm down. I'm going to make bread and then decide what to do."* When you're done kneading say, *"That felt good. I feel calmer now."*
- Ask your child if she would like to make bread to calm down. Say, *"You look hurt because Katherine was mean to you. Would you like to let go of the hurt by kneading bread?"*

✐ *Self-calming tools*

Get a Hug

Olivia is very attached to her dad. Usually when he leaves she has a melt-down. Today, Olivia watched him leave and then came to me, raised her arms and said,"Hug."

Physical touch is comforting for most – but not all – people. Learning to ask for a hug when you want one is a good skill.

How to teach:
- Model asking your spouse or partner for a hug. *"David, I'm feeling sad. Can I have a hug?"* When done, say, *"Thanks. I feel better."*
- Notice if your child likes hugs. If not, you might try holding hands instead.
- Offer a hug when your child is sad. *"Tami, you look sad. Would you like a hug?"*

Drink from a Water Bottle

Jake wanted to play basketball, but he wasn't skilled. He tried to practice but he got frustrated easily and would kick the trash can, spilling the garbage. We told him, "Being mad is okay, and spilling the trash is not. You'll have to find something else to do to relieve your frustration." And he did. Somehow he discovered that taking "water breaks" by sucking water from a water bot-tle helped calm him down.

For many people, adults and children, the act of sucking water from a bottle has a soothing effect, just as sucking soothes infants.

How to teach:
- Model drinking water when you're frustrated. For example, say, *"I need a water break."* After a couple of swigs, say, *"I feel better now."*
- Make "magic" calming juice. Fill a sucking-type water bottle and add a squirt of lemon. Offer, *"Here is some calming juice."*

Take a Warm Bath

Megan, my daughter, is a feisty little red head with quite a temper. The thing that calms her best is water. When I notice feelings are escalating, I will ask, "Looks like you're getting frustrated. Would a bath help you calm down?"

For many people water is soothing. It can be a bubble bath, shower, splashing in water or even listening to a little water fountain. *Note:* Water excites some children rather than calming them.

How to teach:
- Talk about how calm and clean you feel after a bath or shower.
- Reflect how comfortable your child feels when he is done bathing.
- Model changing your feelings. Say, *"I'm so angry that the cooking class is full, I'm going to take a long bath and wash away my irritated feelings."*

Get a Snack

I have noticed that one way Kevin calms himself is by eating something. It can be a cookie, cracker, or piece of fruit.

Food is a form of comfort in all cultures. The food can be a warm beverage or a food. Carbohydrates are particularly useful in generating a mood change. As with all tools, getting a snack is best used with other tools, not relied on as the only source of comfort.

How to teach:
- Model drinking a cup of tea. *"I'm feeling frustrated. I am going to take a break and drink some tea. Then I'm going to go back and figure out this puzzle."*
- Offer your child a glass of warm milk or animal crackers when he is sad.
- If the child says, *"I'm still sad, I need another cookie,"* respond with, *"If you're still sad, try a different tool."*

✑ *Humor tools*

Read Humor Books

We used to have trouble with our son until he learned to read. Now when he is upset with someone, he retreats to his room and reads his joke books. When he is calm, he comes out and we talk about the situation.

Laughter changes the body chemistry and helps dissipate feelings that are eating at us.

How to teach:
- Read jokes and laugh with your child. Notice how different your body feels after you have had a hearty laugh.
- Model reading jokes to calm yourself down. After a difficult phone call you can say, *"I am really upset. I'm going to read some jokes and let go of my anger."* When you are done reading, report back. *"I feel much better after laughing at the silly jokes."*

Watch Funny Videos

My son was furious that he could not use the computer. Usually he sulked until he got what he wanted – sometimes for hours. Today he sat beside me as I watched "TV Bloopers" and within five minutes he had laughed himself into a good humor.

You may want to collect movies or shows that your children find funny.

How to teach:
- Model watching a funny video when you are upset. You could say, *"I'm so frustrated with the computer, I'm making lots of mistakes. I need to calm myself before I continue. I'm going to watch a funny movie."* When you're done, comment on how much better you feel.
- If your child is angry, invite him to watch a funny movie with you. When it's over, ask how he feels.

Find Humor in the Situation

My daughter was having a bad hair day – hair sticking out at odd angles. Instead of bursting into tears as she has in the past, she quipped, "I'm off to school to see if I can set a new hair style."

When you find humor in a difficult situation, the situation becomes more bearable. It helps to look at things from a different angle.

How to teach:
- Share a situation that happened to you at work and how you found humor. For example, *"I had put off calling Mr. Zooinski because I was scared. So today I imagined him sitting in his office in his underwear and I wasn't so scared."*
- Ask your child to help you find humor. When the coffee cake you made for breakfast is hard as a rock, you could say, *"A nickel for the silliest use of this cake."*

Make Silly Faces

Brian has always liked to make faces. Even as a baby his face was very mobile. One day in preschool he discovered that when kids were being mean, he could make a silly face. They would laugh and be friends again.

Laughter is a wonderful way to defuse the tension and bring people together. It is particularly helpful when the humor is kind (not putting anyone down).

How to teach:
- Read *When You're Silly and You Know It* and practice making the silly faces in the book.

- Practice making silly faces. Get mirrors and make more silly faces. See how long you can laugh.
- Model using silly faces or silly dances when you are upset. You could say, *"I'm so frustrated that it rained today, I'm going to do a silly rain-go-away-dance."* Then make up a dance in which you push the rain back up into the sky.

Appendix D

Songs and skits

This appendix contains the text of the song *When You're MAD and You Know It . . .* and two skits referred to in Chapter 6.

When You're Mad and You Know It . . .

Text from the toddler board book of the same title by Elizabeth Crary and Shari Steelsmith.

> When you're mad and you know it, blow air out.
> When you're mad and you know it, shake it out.
> When you're mad and you know it, then your scowl will
>   surely show it.
> When you're mad and you know it, give a shout.
>
> When you're mad and you know it, run with Lad.
> When you're mad and you know it, stomp with Dad.
> When you're mad and you know it, then your scowl will
>   surely show it.
> When you're mad and you know it, say "I'm mad."

Willy & the Wise Owl - Skit

Owl is sitting in a tree sleeping.

Willy   Walks on stage muttering. *Sisters are dumb. All they ever do is get you in trouble. I'd like to toss her in the recycle bin or give her to someone else.*

Owl   Yawns. *What's the trouble, Willie?*

Willy   *Ellie came into MY room. And broke MY Lego spaceship. And whe I tried to push her out of my room, she yelled, "Stop hurting me." And then Mom came and got mad at ME!*

Owl   *Sounds like you're upset that your sister came in your room and broke your spaceship, and you got in trouble.*

Willy   Yeah.

Owl   *Well, what are you going to do?*

Willy   *I want to throw her in the recycle bin, but I'm sure Mom would find her and let her out. And then Mom would be mad at me again.*

Owl   *Probably. Would you like some ideas on how to handle the situation?*

Willy   *Sure.*

Owl   *Well, let me see. It seems like you have two problems. One, how to protect your spaceship and, second, how to let go of your anger at Ellie and your mom.*

Willy   *I guess so. But what I really want is to keep Ellie from messing with my Legos.*

Owl   *Yes, I can see that's a problem. I have three ideas. One, you could find a place to build that she can't reach. Like a table or countertop.*

Willy   *Well, I could try the dining table. She can climb on the chairs, but if I push them way in, it won't be so easy for her. What else?*

Owl   *Ellie may want to play with your Legos just because you are. Some little kids think everything their older brothers do is interesting.*

Willy   *That's possible. She always follows me around.*

Owl   *Is there something Ellie could play with near you that might interest her?*

Willy   *Umm. Err. She could use some extra Legos and make a docking station for the spaceship. If she sat far away that might work.*

Owl   *Another idea is to get help if she goes near your spaceship. Is there someone who could help you?*

Willy   *No. Mom always sides with Ellie, no matter what.*

Owl   *Hmm. Do you think Mom would help take her from your room if you asked?*

Willy   *I don't know. She might.*

Owl   *You have three ideas – working up high, giving her something to do, and calling for help. What do you think will work?*

Willy   *I don't know. Ellie might pull out a chair and climb up to the table. And, she might not want to build something herself, even in my room. And I don't know if Mom will come quick enough when I call.*

Owl   *Well, think about it. It is sometimes hard to tell what will work. Since what you're doing isn't working, these ideas have a better chance. If these don't work, there are many more ideas. You can find an idea that will work.*

Willy   *Okay, I'll think about it. And I'll come back tomorrow and tell you what I've tried.*

Note: This skit has six parts – setting the stage, defining the problem, generating alternatives, evaluating ideas, calling for action and commitment, and finally a closing. You can use this formula (or problem-solving process) to make your own skits and then begin to ask your child for ideas to help the puppets.

Willy, Wise Owl & Wanda the Witch

Wise   Owl and Willy are dozing under a tree.

Wanda   Wanda the witch comes on stage muttering to herself. *I can't find anyone. Where is everyone?* Then she wails. *Nobody wants to play with me.*

Owl   Startles and flies into the tree. Speaking in a menacing voice. *Who dares to startle me from my sleep?*

Wanda   In a timid voice. *I dare. Or at least, I didn't mean to startle you. I – I – I'm sorry.*

Owl   Stares at Wanda intently. *Apology accepted. Now what was that wailing all about?*

Wanda   *Everybody hides from me. Nobody'll be my friend.* Sobs.

Owl   *How odd. You look like a nice witch. Have people always run away from you?*

Wanda   Hangs her head. Responds in an embarrassed voice. *No-o-o.*

Owl   *What happened?*

Wanda   *Well, one day I got mad. Tommy wouldn't pretend to be a dragon for me to ride so I turned him into a frog. Then everybody else ran away. Now whenever they see me they hide. It's not fair. I didn't leave him a frog forever, only for one day.*

Owl   *Yes, I can see you mean well. Why do you think they hide from you?*

Wanda   *Because they don't like me.*

Owl   *Do you think there could be another reason?*

Wanda   *No. They hide whenever I come by.*

Owl   *When did it start?*

Wanda   Thinks a moment. *Right after I turned Tommy into a frog?*

Owl   *How would you like it if I turned you into a frog?*

Wanda   *I wouldn't like it.* Angrily. *I'd turn you into a cherry and eat you.*

Owl   Imperiously. *Wanda!*

Wanda   *I'm sorry.* Hangs her head.

Owl   *Back to my question. Wanda, would you like me to turn you into a frog?*

Wanda   *No, sir.*

Owl   *If you were not a witch, what would you do if you thought I was going to turn you into a frog?*

Wanda   *I don't know. If I wasn't a witch, I might run away and hide from you. Oh.*

Owl   *Why would you run away?*

Wanda *Because I don't want to be a frog.*

Owl   *Not because you don't like me?*

Wanda *No.*

Owl   *Wanda, it seems to me you have two problems. One, you need to apologize for turning Tommy into a frog . . .*

Wanda Angrily. *How can I do that if he runs away?*

Owl   Ignoring Wanda . . . *and, you need to learn ways to calm yourself so you can negotiate with your friends.*

Wanda *What's ne-go-ti-ate?*

Owl   *It's finding ideas that both you and your friend like.*

Wanda *Oh. Can I do that?*

Owl   *You can learn. First you need to learn three ways to calm yourself.*

Wanda *What do I do?*

Owl   *Ask Willie.*

Willy   Willie peeks from behind the tree. In a panicked voice. *Me?*

Owl   *Yes, you. Willie, tell her how you calm yourself when you are mad at your sister or mother.*

At this point, ask your child to play Willie puppet and to teach the witch how to calm herself.

If your child has trouble thinking of ideas in the beginning, Owl can ask "Willie" questions like "*What did you do yesterday when you were so mad at . . . ?*" Or, "*What did Katie try in the book* I'm Mad *that you read?*" Or, "*What might you do if you had magic powers?*" The goal is to get your child thinking of ideas.

Appendix E

Resources

These are books about feelings and problem solving for children and informational books for parents. The parent books include books on brainstorming, general parenting, de-cluttering and organization, bullying and violence prevention, temperament, and emotional competence.

Children's books on feelings and problem solving

♥ Feelings books – identify feelings and how they change.
◆ Problem-solving books – offer ways to deal with feelings and situations.

♥ *All My Feelings at Home: Ellie's Day* (1989) and *All My Feelings at Preschool: Nathan's Day* (1991) both by Susan Levine Friedman and Susan Conlin. Each page in these stories asks questions to make the feelings relevant to the listener. Seattle: Parenting Press.

◆ Children's Problem Solving Series: *I Want It, I Can't Wait, I Want to Play, My Name Is Not Dummy, I'm Lost* and *Mommy, Don't Go* by Elizabeth Crary. Seattle: Parenting Press, 1996.

♥◆ Dealing with Feelings Series: *I'm Frustrated* (1992), *I'm Mad* (1992), *I'm Proud* (1992), *I'm Excited* (1994), *I'm Furious* (1994) and *I'm Scared* (1994) by Elizabeth Crary. Each book offers a variety of options and shows the possible results of those choices. Seattle: Parenting Press.

◆ Decision Is Yours Series: *Finders, Keepers?* by Elizabeth Crary (1987), *Bully on the Bus* by Carl W. Bosch (1988), *Making the Grade* by Carl W. Bosch (1991), *First Day Blues* by Peggy King Anderson (1992) and *Under Whose Influence?* by Judy Laik (1994). Seattle: Parenting Press.

♥◆ Feelings for Little Children Series: When *You're Mad and You Know It, When You're Happy and You Know It, When You're Silly and You Know It,* and *When You're Shy and You Know It* by Elizabeth Crary and Shari Steelsmith. Each board book offers toddlers age-appropriate ways to express their feelings. Seattle: Parenting Press, 1996.

♦ Kids Can Choose Series: *Heidi's Irresistible Hat, Amy's Disappearing Pickle,* and *Willie's Noisy Sister* by Elizabeth Crary. Seattle: Parenting Press, 2001.

♥ *The Way I Feel* by Janan Cain. Simple verse and compelling color illustrations help children identify and deal with feelings. Seattle: Parenting Press, 2001.

♥ *What Is A Feeling?* by David Krueger. Distinguishes between emotions and body sensations. Seattle: Parenting Press, 1993.

Feeling games and activities

Feeling Elf Cards by Elizabeth Crary and Peaco Todd. Seattle: Parenting Press, 2003. The deck consists of 12 game cards and 40 feeling elf cards in color, 20 elves with the name of the feeling on the card and the same 20 elves without the feeling word.

Brainstorming or idea books

365 Wacky, Wonderful Ways to Get Your Child to Do What You Want by Elizabeth Crary. Seattle: Parenting Press, 1995.

Help! For Parents of Children from Birth to Five by Jean Illsley Clarke, et al. San Francisco: HarperCollins, 1993.

Help! For Parents of School-Aged Children and Teens by Jean Illsley Clarke, et al. San Francisco: HarperCollins, 1993.

Love & Limits: Guidance Tools for Creative Parenting by Elizabeth Crary. Seattle: Parenting Press, 1994.

Other parenting resources

Growing Up Again: Parenting Ourselves, Parenting Our Children by Jean Illsley Clarke and Connie Dawson. Center City, Minn.: Hazelden Information & Educational Services, 1998.

Kids Can Cooperate: A Practical Guide to Teaching Problem Solving by Elizabeth Crary. Seattle: Parenting Press, 1984.

Pick Up Your Socks . . . and Other Skills Growing Children Need! by Elizabeth Crary. Seattle: Parenting Press, 1990.

Self-Esteem: A Family Affair by Jean Illsley Clarke. Center City, Minn.: Hazelden Information & Educational Services, 1998.

The Too Precious Child: The Perils of Being a Super-Parent and How to Avoid Them by Lynne H. William, et al. New York: Simon & Schuster, 1987.

Without Spanking or Spoiling: A Practical Approach to Toddler and Preschool Guidance, second edition, by Elizabeth Crary. Seattle: Parenting Press, 1993.

Organizational skills

Clutter Free! Finally and Forever by Don Aslett. Pocatello, Idaho: Marsh Creek Press, 1995.

Getting Organized: The Easy Way to Put Your Life in Order by Stephanie Winston. New York: Warner Books, 1991.

The Personal Efficiency Program: How to Get Organized to Do More Work in Less Time by Kerry L. Gleeson. New York: John Wiley & Sons, 2000.

Bullying and violence prevention

Aggressors, Victims, and Bystanders by Ron Slaby. Newton, Mass.: Education Development Center, 1997.

Bullies and Victims: Helping Your Child Through the Schoolyard Battlefield by Suellen Fried and Paula Fried. New York: M. Evans, 1998.

Bullies: From the Playground to the Boardroom by Jane Middelton-Moz and Mary Lee Zawadski. Deerfield Beach, Fla.: Health Communications, 2002.

Early Violence Prevention: Tools for Teachers of Young Children by Ron Slaby. Washington, D.C.: National Association for the Education of Young Children, 1995.

Easing the Teasing: Helping Your Child Cope with Name-Calling, Ridicule, and Verbal Bullying by Judy S. Freedman. Chicago: Contemporary Books, 2002.

How to Handle Bullies, Teasers, and Other Meanies: A Book That Takes the Nuisance Out of Name Calling and Other Nonsense by Kate Cohen-Posey. Highland City, Fla.: Rainbow Books, 1995.

Sexual Harassment and Teens: A Program for Positive Change by Susan Strauss and Pamela Espeland. Minneapolis: Free Spirit Publishing, 1992.

Violence Prevention Resource Guide for Parents by Peggy Patten and Anne S. Robertson. Champaign, Ill.: ERIC/EECE Publications, 2001.

Temperament

Living with the Active Alert Child: Groundbreaking Strategies for Parents, third edition, by Linda S. Budd. Seattle: Parenting Press, 2003.

Temperament Tools: Working with Your Child's Inborn Traits by Helen Neville and Diane Clark Johnson. Seattle: Parenting Press, 1998.

Understanding Temperament: Strategies for Creating Family Harmony by Lyndall Shick. Seattle: Parenting Press, 1998.

Emotional competence

Emotional Intelligence by Daniel Goleman. New York: Bantam Books, 1995.

Emotional Literacy: To Be a Different Kind of Smart by Rob Bocchino. Thousand Oaks, Calif.: Corwin Press, 1999.

Protecting the Gift: Keeping Children and Teenagers Safe (and Partners Sane) by Gavin de Becker. New York: Dell Books, 2000.

Raising an Emotionally Intelligent Child by John Gottman and Joan Declaire. New York: Simon & Schuster, 1998.

Working with Emotional Intelligence by Daniel Goleman. New York: Bantam Doubleday Dell Publishing, 2000.

Your Child's Emotional Health: Adolescence by Jack Maguire. New York: Macmillan, 1995.

Index

A

Academic trouble, 8, 99
Acknowledging effort, 19
Acknowledging feelings, 9, 16, 17, 31
Act effectively, 44
Action plan, 88, 90
Activities to teach coping with feelings, 114-124
Activities to teach about feelings, 30, 101-113
Age, developmental, 95; to start teaching about feelings, 64, 97
Aggression, 8, 99
Alcohol addiction, 8, 100
Anger, as warning, 9, 82-83, 88, 90, 97, 99
Apologizing, 80
Ask for a decision, 53
Auditory/verbal tools to express/cope with feelings, 34, 114, 116-118

B

Back out and let child cope, 39, 98
Bedtime, 70; routine, 91
Books, use of: to introduce feelings, 23, 65, 70, 118, 129; to introduce laughter, 35
Brainstorming, 44, 45, 88, 90; books, 130
Bullying, 49

C

Calm, staying, 76-93
Calming strategies, 86, 87
Change or move, 49
Changes, making, 67
Charts: 101 Feeling words, 24; Affirmations, 84; Basic feelings vocabulary, 68; Dealing with feelings, 19; Discounting, 30-31; Handling a situation, 17; Lynn's action plan, 91; Parents' role changes as children grow, 15; Review of how to teach self-calming tools, 96; Self-calming strategies, 36; STAR problem-solving summary, 44, 58
Children's books on feelings and problem solving, 129
Choices, offering, 15
Clarify the situation, 49
Closing summary 98
Clutter, reducing, 87-88
Comfort, appropriate, 42
Comforting child, 15
Creative tools to express/cope with feelings, 35, 114, 119-121
Crisis, what to do in, 14, 16-21

D

Depression, 8, 100
Develop vocabulary, activities for, 101-103

Discounting feelings, 30-31
Distract or divert, 50
Do something unexpected, 50
Drug addiction, 8, 100

E

Eating disorders, 8, 100
Emotional competence, books, 132
Emotional illiteracy, cost of, 8, 99-100
Emotional reserves, lack of, 75
Emotional sensitivity, 94
Emotional triggers, 77
Emotions, teaching about, 9-10; separating parent's and child's, 78-80
Evaluate ideas, 53
Exercise, physical, 90
Exercises: Action plan, 93; Action plan worksheet, 92; Changing self-talk, 85; Children's self-calming tools, 37; Dealing with a crisis, 18; Dealing with a tantrum, 21; Feelings skills inventory, 64; Feelings vocabulary, 23; Identify graded feelings, 25; Identifying feelings and events, 62-63; Identifying responses, 66; Identifying your parenting EQ style, 13; Make a plan, 74; Notice how emotions feel, 25; Plan how to teach a calming tool, 41; Record calming tools, 34; Skills inventory–nature of feelings, 28; Strategies to deal with people, 51; Strategies to deal with things, 48; What is your parenting EQ style?, 11-12; Who's in charge of the feelings?, 81; Who's sorry now?, 79; Working to avoid a crisis, 20
Expand language, 68
Experiences, child's, 95

F

Family routines and rituals, 68
Fear, a warning, 9, 30
Feeling Elf Cards, 69
Feeling games and activities, 130
Feeling lovable/capable, 82
Feeling word of the day, 67-68
Feelings: acceptableness of, 26, 30; change, 9, 26, 68, 70; comfortable and uncomfortable, 23, 24, 29; coping with, 23, 29, 56-66, 90, 114-124; different from actions, 9, 17, 27, 70; expressing appropriately, 15; gradations of, 24-25; identifying, 23; ignoring, 31; in charge of, 80; labeling, 15, 16, 23, 32; nature of, 23, 26, 28; physical signs of, 23, 25; responding to kids', 10, 56-66; teaching about, 56-66; suppressing, 25; variety of, 24, 27; vocabulary, 9, 19, 22-25, 101, 102-103
Feelings cards, 69
Feelings dial, 30, 68, 69, 105
Finger puppets, 70, 106
Focus, on event, 57; on feeling, 57
Food, calming effect of, 35
Friends, dealing with, 60-61

G

Gather data, 52
General calming strategies, 87
Generate ideas, 52
Get help, 50

H

Happiness, responsibility for, 7-8; child's role, 8; parents' role, 8, 10
High/low point of day, 68-69
Homework, 69
Humor to express/cope with feelings, 35-37, 114, 122-124

I

Identify choices, activities for, 101, 109-111
Identify feelings, activities for, 101, 103-105
Identify problem and needed skills, 72, 75
Ignore the problem, 31, 49
"I'm sorry", 79
In charge of feelings, 80-81
Instant calming strategies, 86
Intensity, 94, 97
Involvement, parents', 80
IQ, 99
Issues, parental, 77-78

J

Journal, of feelings, 70

K

Know other people have feelings, activities for, 101, 111-113

L

Labeling feelings, 32
Language concepts, need for, 50-51; expand, 67
Laughter, to reduce stress, 35
Learning a new skill, 47, 48
Listen and pay attention, 50-51

M

Mealtime, 68
Meltdowns, what to do during, 10, 14, 18, 38, 64, 87, 88
Mentor, for feelings, 97
Modeling, parental, 8, 27, 29, 35, 39, 45, 69, 70, 71, 95
Mood, 94
Music, use of, 90

N

Negotiating, differences, 49, 50-54; steps in, 52-54, 80; teaching, 51-54

O

Observations to teach feelings, 29
Options, 15
Order, create/maintain, 88
Organizational skills, books, 131

P

Parent as, coach, 15, 40, 55, comforter, 15, 40, 54, consultant, 15, 40, 55, teacher, 15, 40, 54
Parental support, 9-10, 14-21, 40, 54-55
Parenting resources, books, 130
Parenting style, coaching, 13, critical, 13, fixing, 13, sensitive, 13
People, dealing with, 46, 49-50, 61
Physical signs of feelings, 25
Physical tools to express/cope with feelings, 34, 114, 115-116
Planning, 71-76
Practicing, 75
Pretend, 38-39, 72, 96
Problem solving, steps to, 43-45; teaching, 57-65

Problems, challenging, 71, 75
Professional help, getting, 97-98
Prompt child, 39, 72
"Put the lid on" feelings, 9, 25
"Putting a child together", 34, 116

R
Reframe the situation, 49
Resolving problems, 20
Responsibility for dealing with
    feelings, 15, 39
Retry situation, 73
Review & revise, 45
Review the situation, 75

S
Self-calming tools, 34-37, 39;
    teaching, 37-40; to
    express/cope with feelings,
    114, 121-122
Self-esteem, 82
Self-soothing skills, 19, 37
Self-talk, 84-85
Separate feelings and actions,
    activities for, 101, 107-109
Situation skills, 17, 19, 27, 28, 88
Skills, lack of, 46, 47; teaching,
    72, 76
STAR parenting, 89
STAR problem-solving process,
    44, 58
State the problem, 52
Stop & focus, 43
Stories, to teach feelings, 30
Strategies, teaching, 18
Stress, reducing, 19, 35, 77
Stress bucket, 19
Support, levels of, 9, 14, 15

T
Tables: Brainstorming for ideas to
    handle a situation, 89;
    "General" or preventive calm-
    ing strategies, 87; "Instant"
    calming strategies, 86
Take care of yourself, 83-87
Tantrums, 14, 19, 90
Tasks, breaking into small pieces,
    39
Teens, 16, 100
Teaching about feelings, 30, 57,
    by modeling, 29, by observa-
    tions, 29, by stories, 30, 97
Teaching about problem solving,
    57
Temperament, 33, 94-95, 97;
    books, 131
Testosterone, 96
Things, dealing with, 46-48
Think of ideas, 44
Tools, for coping with feelings,
    114-124; introducing, 38,
    linking, 38, practicing, 39,
    prompting, 39
Transitions, 68
Two fish story, 72

U
Understand feelings change, activ-
    ities for, 101, 105-107
Understanding, lack of, 46; need
    for, 51
Use force, 50
Use humor, 50

V

Videos, to introduce feelings
vocabulary, 23, 30, 65; to
introduce laughter, 35; to
reduce stress, 35
Violence prevention, books, 131
Visual tools to express/cope with
feelings, 35, 114, 118-119
Vocabulary, 22-25; activities to
develop, 101, 102-103

W

"When You're Mad and You Know
It," song, 125
Whose problem?, 78
Willy & the Wise Owl skit, 125-
127
Willy, Wise Owl & Wanda the
Witch skit, 127-128
Work, teaching takes, 95-96

Your notes

Your notes

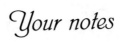

Your notes

Your notes

Your notes

More books for helping kids deal with disappointment